the **TRIBE** GUIDE

thetriibe.com

PUBLISHER

Morgan Elise Johnson

EDITOR-IN-CHIEF

Tiffany Walden

HEAD OF OPERATIONS

David Elutilo

ART DIRECTORS

Robin Carnilius

Ash Lane

EDITORS

Benét J. Wilson

Jim Daley

ASSISTANT TO THE PUBLISHER

Nia Ali

COPY EDITORS

Jillian Melero

Alex Perry

WRITERS

Kelly Hayes   Matt Harvey   Fawn Pochel   Kelly Garcia
Tonia Hill   Arionne Nettles   Crystal Hill
Corli Jay   Natalie Frazier   Ade D. Adeniji   Lindsey Wright
Bella BAHHS   Monroe Anderson   Damon Williams

PHOTOGRAPHERS

Darius Griffin   Alexander Gouletas   Ash Lane
Tyger Ligon   Sterling Hightower

RESEARCH & OUTREACH

Anthony Bryant

INDIGENOUS CONSULTANT

Jonathan Ballew

ISBN: 979-8-88890-195-3

Special thanks to the Chicago History Museum for the archival photos.
Cover photo of Kannon Purnell shot by Ash Lane.

The TRiiBE is a digital media platform that is reshaping the narrative of Black Chicago and giving ownership back to the people. Our original works in journalism and documentary, alongside creative writing and video, capture the multifaceted essence of the Black experience in pursuit of truth and liberation.

 @thetriibechicago    @TheTRiiBE   @thetriibe    @thetriibechicago

 HaymarketBooks

CONTENTS

EDITOR'S NOTE

Originally published in summer 2021

I didn't learn much about Black Chicago history in school. It wasn't taught to us in the same ways that we learned about Black history moments such as slavery, the Great Migration, the Harlem Renaissance and the Civil Rights Movement. Chairman Fred Hampton walked the same West Side streets I did as a kid, yet I didn't learn about him and the Black Panther Party until I was grown. And it wasn't until I was well into my 20s — around when I started *The TRiiBE* — that I read *An Autobiography of Black Chicago* by Dempsey J. Travis, which taught me about the free and formerly enslaved Black folks who lived in what's now the affluent downtown and South Loop areas of the city — this was well before emancipation in 1865, and at least two decades before major fires decimated the budding Black communities.

I went to majority-Black schools for most of my life: St. Catherine-St. Lucy for grammar school, and Providence St. Mel for high school. As we've recently come into the modern Movement for Black Lives, there has been more of an internal push for teachers to stray from the textbooks to teach hidden Black history gems. But for me growing up in the 1990s, my teachers never deviated from the history textbook to teach us our Chicago roots.

We are the legacy of resilient people who routinely did the impossible: fled oppression, built community, created institutions, transformed the culture and fought endlessly for our right to exist.

For this issue of *The TRiiBE Guide*, we wanted to center our history. We wanted to turn this Heritage Edition of the magazine into an introduction to the Black and Indigenous Chicago history that many of us weren't taught in school. History is often told from the viewpoint of the oppressor — the colonizers and settlers who record history in ways that present them as the winner. Because of this, the history of the oppressed is lost or erased in its entirety. That's the biggest challenge we faced as we tried to tell Chicago's Indigenous story, and it's unfortunately the reason we don't have many Indigenous moments that don't include colonialism or war in this magazine.

While researching the descendants of John Jones and his wife Mary Jane Richardson Jones, two abolitionists and pioneers of Black Chicago, I found Dr. Bruce Purnell. He is the third great-grandson of the Joneses, and is well aware of the impact his ancestors have had on the world. In our interviews with him over the phone, he said something that really stuck with me: it's important to understand your "why" and to not have that narrative spoon-fed to you by your oppressor.

As Dr. Purnell's young grandson, Kannon Purnell, graces the cover of this magazine, I think back on my childhood: being in school, learning a history that was created by the oppressor. As with the Jones family, who passed down their history from generation to generation, it's so important for us to tap into our African roots of oral and written tradition and educate our families and our youth about our history. We can no longer allow the American system, which robbed us of our lands and bodies, to teach us our story. There's liberation in owning our own story.

TIFFANY WALDEN
Editor-in-chief

Shabbona, a Potawatomi chief

The Native American Village at A Century of Progress, also known as the Chicago World's Fair

WE BEEN HERE
Before 1837

Archival photos courtesy of the Chicago History Museum

I, WE BEEN HERE

BEFORE 1837

BY MATT HARVEY

See, here's the thing: No matter what the history books may tell you about Chicago, the Indigenous peoples have been here. There would be no Chicago without them.

Their journey begins way back, when the land we now call home was inhabited by the Potawatomi, Miami, Ojibwe, Odawa and Illini Confederation. At various points in time, each tribe had bands who settled the area or traded with other Indigenous tribes along Chicago's River Valley. Since most of their history is passed down orally, much of it has been stolen or erased by the same European and new American colonizers who stole their lands.

Therefore, facts about the Indigenous tribes on the land we call Chicago are heavily debated, and often confined to the parameters of what non-Indigenous people, such as French Jesuit missionary Jacques Marquette and fur trader Louis Joliet, wrote in their journals.

According to John N. Low, a citizen of the Pokagon Band of Potawatomi Indians and an American Indian Studies professor at Ohio State University, the elders say his tribe are descendants of the mound builders, prehistoric Indigenous inhabitants who built earth mounds for religious, ceremonial and burial practices. The site of one such mound is in Cahokia, Ill., an ancient settlement that dates back more than 1,000 years before European contact.

Make no mistake — this land's history begins with Indigenous people. If not for Kitihawa, the Potawatomi woman who married Jean Baptiste Pointe DuSable, he wouldn't have been able to build the beginnings of the city we know today.

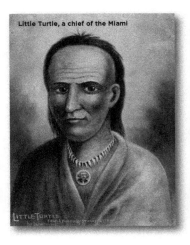
Little Turtle, a chief of the Miami

1794

The Battle of Fallen Timbers in 1794 was the last stand of the Northwestern Confederacy against the U.S. With the help of British-Canadian forces, the battle ended in a stalemate. The Treaty of Greenville ended the war, but opened the door for further U.S. expansion and genocide of Native tribes.

Detail portrait of Jean Baptiste Pointe

1783

In 1783, Indigenous tribes of the Great Lakes region joined forces to create the Northwestern Confederacy in order to fight back against America's westward expansion in the Northwest Indian War. The tribes who lived on the land we call Chicago — such as the Miami, Kickapoo, Illini and Potawatomi — were all part of the Northwestern Confederacy.

1778

In 1778, Jean Baptiste Pointe DuSable, an African-French trader born in Haiti and educated in France, traveled north from New Orleans along the Mississippi River to Illinois. DuSable was married to a Potawatomi woman named Kitihawa about whom little information is known (the folks documenting history at the time were extremely sexist). Kitihawa's lineage made it safe for them to establish a settlement on Potawatomi land near the mouth of the Chicago River. The construction of their home officially made DuSable the first non-Indigenous permanent resident of what we now call Chicago.

The signing of the Treaty of Greenville in 1794 marked a tipping point in the fight for Indigenous tribes to keep their land. In the treaty, the Northwest Confederacy of Indigenous tribes ceded most of their land in what we now call Ohio, as well as large tracts in Illinois, Indiana and Michigan. In 1830, President Andrew Jackson signed the Indian Removal Act, which forced Indigenous tribes off of their ancestral land in the Midwest onto the land west of the Mississippi River. During this time, Leopold Pokagon, the tribal leader of the Saint Joseph River Valley Potawatomi, was on his way to Detroit to meet with the Detroit Diocese. If Leopold could get a Catholic priest to come and convert his tribe to Christianity, it might serve them well in their struggle to maintain their land. Leopold was successful, and the tribe's conversion

The Last Council of the Pottawatomies, 1833

wasn't just superficial either; the Saint Joseph River Valley Potawatomi became practicing Catholics. In 1833, the U.S. government called together all of the Potawatomi tribes of the area to a final treaty negotiation at Chicago to establish the terms of removal under the Indian Removal Act. Among the invited leaders was Leopold Pokagon, who negotiated an amendment to the act allowing the Saint Joseph River Valley Potawatomi to keep part of their land. The Saint Joseph River Valley Potawatomi became known as the Pokagon Band Potawatomi after their Wkema (leader).

1800

In May of 1800, DuSable sold all of his land on the Chicago settlement to a French interpreter named Jean La Lime, who bought it on behalf of a Canadian named William Burnett. The sale was witnessed by John Kinzie, Burnett's homeboy, who later purchased the property from La Lime. DuSable and Kitihawa moved their family to St. Charles, Mo. The reason why a businessman and trader like DuSable suddenly sold such a settlement at a prime location at the mouth of the river is still unknown.

1812

During the War of 1812, Indigenous forces resisting westward colonization planned attacks on Midwest settlements, including Chicago. One of those attacks was the Battle of Fort Dearborn, in which a group of Potawotami warriors ambushed Fort Dearborn evacuees who'd heard that an attack was coming. The Potawotami won the battle and destroyed the fort.

1818

DuSable died in St. Charles, Mo., on Aug. 28, 1818, where he lived and worked as a ferry operator on the Missouri River.

1837

The City of Chicago was incorporated on March 4, 1837 with three distinct regions written into its charter that were separated by the Chicago River; the North, South, and West Sides.

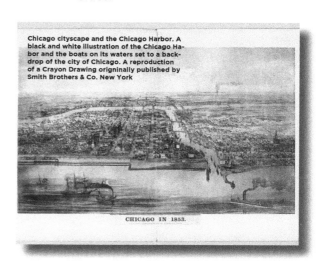

Chicago cityscape and the Chicago Harbor. A black and white illustration of the Chicago Harbor and the boats on its waters set to a backdrop of the city of Chicago. A reproduction of a Crayon Drawing originally published by Smith Brothers & Co. New York

CHICAGO IN 1853.

THE SETTLEMENT THAT DUSABLE BUILT

By Matt Harvey

Originally published in summer 2021

Jean Baptiste Pointe DuSable's settlement at the mouth of the Chicago River is the heart from which the city of Chicago was built. As time passed, and ownership of the land changed, its history has been smudged, so much so that most people had no idea he lived there until the mid 20th century. DuSable, Kitihawa and their children first showed up in future Chicago during the 1780s. They built a five-bedroom home, a horse mill, a bake house, a dairy, a smokehouse, a poultry house, a workshop, a stable, a barn, an orchard, and huts for DuSable's employees. The family lived and worked on this land for at least a decade. It is unclear why DuSable moved his family to St. Charles, Missouri, where he ended up living a modest life as a ferry operator.

The story gets stranger when you look at the circumstances surrounding the purchase, and how they might've led to Chicago's first murder. Jean La Lime, an agent of a Canadian named William Burnett, bought the estate from DuSable in 1800. The sale was filed in Detroit, and witnessed by John Kinzie, a fur trader and Burnett's business partner. Kinzie, who became infamous for his shady business practices, gained ownership of the land from La Lime under murky circumstances that didn't sit right with La Lime. Kinzie built a mansion on the property. Kinzie and La Lime's beef escalated into a fight where Kinzie killed La Lime on June 17, 1812. The cause for the murder is disputed but it's suspected that La Lime was threatening to expose Kinzie's shady dealings in land acquisition and illegal trading at Fort Dearborn. Considering that the only people who knew of DuSable's ownership of the property were traders who'd passed through, and the Indigenous people who were being systematically murdered and displaced, killing La Lime meant that Kinzie could bolster his reputation as the so-called "Father of Chicago."

The false title stuck. The site where DuSable built the first settlement in Chicago was recognized as "Kinzie Mansion," and Kinzie's family was hailed as Chicago's first family. This misconception was treated as fact for much of Chicago's history and was first debunked by the Black women-led National De Saible Memorial Society at the 1933 Chicago World's Fair.

See's House

The Temple Building 1833
A Church Building used by several Denominations

Sam Miller's Public House

Wolf Tavern

NORTH BRANCH

The TOWN
Popula

Forest

Mr James Farm

1st Public School

Calhoun's House

1st Catholic Church

Parker's House

Blackee House

First Draw-Bridge
Built in 1834 at Dearborn St.

Mail Service
This Road once a
from Niles, Mich.

Second Fort Dearborn
built in 1816

U.S. GOVERNMENT
RESERVATION

Fort Cemetery

GREEN BAY ROAD

Ouilmette

Billy
Sau

DuSable's House

CHICAGO RIVER

Channel cut by
Soldiers in 1833

H I G A N

THE HISTORY OF SEGREGATION STARTS WITH FORCED REMOVAL

By Fawn E. Pochel

Originally published in summer 2021

The nexus of racial segregation and housing disparity in the U.S. continues to perpetuate the characteristics of American Indian removal and chattel slavery. As a direct result of American imperialism, diaspora has become a unique aspect of Black and Indigenous identity.

My diasporic identity formed on my ancestral lands. My father is a survivor of Canada's Sixties Scoop — in which welfare agents removed Indigenous children from their homes and placed them with white foster families — and was adopted by a Midwest farming family in central Illinois. At 11 years old, I experienced displacement first-hand as my family was gentrified out of our home in Avondale.

By the time I was 13 years old, my family was pushed out of Chicago. I returned to Chicago in my early 20s and founded Chi-Nations Youth Council (CNYC) in 2012 with my older sisters and former members of Urban Natives of Chicago and Chi-Society — two Chicago-based Native youth groups that had disbanded.

We founded Chi-Nations with the mission to create safe-space for Native youth. In order to put theory into practice, CNYC works to acknowledge its members' shared history and individual experiences.

"I am well aware that the police see me as a Black man, which automatically makes me a threat. Being both Black and Native, I have had the talk more times than I can count,"

said Anthony Tamez-Pochel, vice-chair of the Youth Advisory Board at the Center for Native American Youth and the neighborhood and business services coordinator at the 33rd Ward. He's also my nephew.

"I was raised in a Native household, which instilled in me the importance of knowing my history which is an ongoing legacy of resistance against continuous reiterations of racist rules and regulations meant to exploit and exterminate me," he added.

American claims over Natives' lands and Native people's lives are wholly dependent on legal fiction and "white supremacist fairy tales," according to Janie Pochel, my sister and an auntie of Chi-Nations Youth Council.

In 1537, Pope Paul III issued a papal bull, "Sublimis Deus," opposing the enslavement of Indigenous peoples. However, the Spanish and French who colonized North America ignored it, and in 1709 the French colonizers formally legalized slavery for Indigenous people.

Under the "Doctrine of Discovery" adopted in 1823 by the U.S. Supreme Court in *Johnson v. M'Intosh*, a unanimous decision led by Chief Justice John Marshall, who wrote in the decision that Christian European nations had assumed "ultimate dominion" over the

lands of America during the Age of Discovery, and that — upon "discovery" — the Native people had lost "their rights to complete sovereignty, as independent nations," and only retained a right of "occupancy" in their lands.

European colonial powers and the U.S. government created American landowners and generational privilege by stealing Indigenous land and enslaving Africans. Settler colonialism in America caused irreparable harm to the peoples and landscapes of Africa and the Americas. Since the first American colony was founded, the state has participated in separating people from their ancestral lands while profiting from their suffering. Today, gentrification has become another physical manifestation of our settler state.

During the summer of 2020, Albany Park was spotlighted after a leftist community group advocated for the development of a community garden at a lot located on Lawrence and Central Park avenues that will be developed into affordable housing by Celadon Holdings LLC. Celadon is run by Scott Henry and Thad Garver, two former executives of JPMorgan.

Albany Park is a historic village and trading site. Today, there is a large Native population in the area and it's the site of three Native

" DON'T COME AT ME SAYING 'HOUSING IS A HUMAN RIGHT' AND THEN ADVOCATE TO GIVE MONEY TO DEVELOPERS TO GENTRIFY OUR COMMUNITIES.

community organizations. Albany Park is also the home of the First Nations Garden, located at Wilson Avenue and Pulaski Road, which my family co-founded with CNYC. My family, like so many others, has recently been gentrified out of Albany Park due to increasing rents.

JPMorgan Chase & Co., the U.S.'s largest bank and parent company of J.P. Morgan, has a long history of racially discriminatory lending practices. In 2017, 49 years after the federal Fair Housing Act banned racial discrimination in lending, the bank agreed to pay a $55 million settlement for offenses of modern-day redlining that took place between 2006 and 2009 and broke laws under the Fair Housing Act and the Equal Credit Opportunity Act.

"Don't come at me saying 'housing is a human right' and then advocate to give money to developers to gentrify our communities," Dr. Sophia Marjanovic, Oglala Lakota, wrote on Facebook. CNCY met Dr. Majanovic in Washington, D.C., and learned about her fight for stronger protections for survivors of domestic violence, rape, human trafficking, sexual assault and harrassment through lobbying.

"The housing disparities I'm seeing in Albany Park due to gentrification is the new iteration of forced removal and racism," said Adrien "A.J." Pochel, a member of Chi-Nations Youth Council and my nephew.

Pochel added that reserves, reservations, ghettos and slums are all a direct result of legal displacement and policing.

"The ability and access to own and acquire property and lands continues to be a barrier for anyone who ain't white," A.J. Pochel said. At the center of racial segregation, displacement and policing are ongoing efforts to protect whiteness in America.

The Last Council of the Pottawatomies, 1833

Portrait of No-in-Ko, a Native American medicine man, at the centennial encampment of Winnebago and Sac-Fox Indians in Lincoln Park in Chicago.

"WHITE SUPREMACY IS AN AMERICAN PROBLEM CREATED BY WHITE PEOPLE.

"America has always been against my people. The first time my race was introduced to school, the slogan was 'Kill the Indian, Save the Man' and many people still carry traumas from those days," said Windfield WoundedEye, a member of Chi-Nations Youth Council. "Many ancestors were kept in those schools and were never the same coming out of them."

It's been more than six decades since the Supreme Court declared "separate but equal" schools unconstitutional in *Brown v. Board of Education*. However, Chicago Public Schools (CPS) remains an example of how heavily segregated modern public education is.

In 1963, 200,000 Chicagoans boycotted CPS as a reaction to the segregationist policies of then-Superintendent Benjamin Willis. Fast forward to 2013, when Mayor Rahm Emanuel

announced an unprecedented 50 school closures, mainly displacing thousands of Black and brown schoolchildren and teachers.

The combination of gentrification, segregation and displacement may seem more complicated than they appear. However, these ongoing events and policies are the evolution of racist ideologies including manifest destiny which absolves America of the atrocities caused by the systematic disenfranchisement of BIPOC people. Urban Natives are absent within America's collective imagination by design — white settler colonial denial erases our occupation of and relationships to our ancestral lands, such as Chicago.

"White supremacy is an American problem created by white people," Tamez-Pochel said. "They need to stop relying on us to do all the labor and face all the consequences of abolishing whiteness."

Haiti Building at the World's Columbian Exposition, Chicago, Illinois, 1893.

African American janitors of the Columbian Guard at the World's Columbian Exposi-

PUTTING DOWN ROOTS
1837 – 1900

American journalist and civil rights activist, Ida B. Wells, 1920

II: PUTTING DOWN ROOTS

1837-1900

BY MATT HARVEY

The first non-Indigenous person to set up shop in Chicago was a Black man named Jean Baptiste Pointe DuSable. Together with his Potowatami wife, Kitihawa, they built their family home: a permanent farm and trading post on the Chicago River, where they lived with their two children.

The white man who later bought their spot — a Canadian fur trader named John Kinzie — was initially credited as the "pioneer who founded Chicago." There used to be a plaque located at 401 Michigan Avenue that marked the former location of DuSable's home, but called the place Kinzie Mansion instead. It's like erasure and gentrification are baked into the city's DNA. Most Chicagoans didn't even start recognizing DuSable as Chicago's first settler until the 1930s.

By Chicago's incorporation as a town on Aug. 12, 1833, the city was a beacon for those seeking new opportunities. Tons of (stolen) land up for grabs, new construction, emerging railroad and transportation systems, and shipping ports along the river and lake turned what was once grassy plains and forests into a burgeoning economic and commercial hub.

Meanwhile, newly freed and freedom-seeking Black folks sought refuge from oppressive states in the deep South and Southeast, where Black people were still in bondage. As Chicago became the bustling new town at the north end of the Underground Railroad enroute to Canada, slowly but surely, Black people turned Chicago into a haven for revolutionaries, abolitionists, entrepreneurs and more.

Potawatomi chief Simon Pokagon—who would deliver a speech at the 1893 Columbian Exposition—fought to keep the city's Indigenous roots alive, and met with President Abraham Lincoln twice to demand the U.S. pay for land taken in the 1833 Treaty of Chicago.

1838

In 1838, Chief Menominee provided shelter to central Indiana Potawatomi who refused to give up their ancestral lands following the enactment of treaties that forced Indigenous people west of the Mississippi river. In the fall, Menominee was among 859 Potawatomi who were forcibly removed from their land in Indiana on Sept. 4, 1838, and marched to Osowatamie, Kansas where they arrived two months later on Nov. 4. Throughout the march, 41 Potawatomie people died and were buried in unmarked graves along t trail. This march became known as the Potawatomi Trail Death.

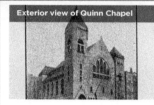

Exterior view of Quinn Chapel

1847

Little by little, freedom-seeking Black folks from the South and freemen from the East settled in on the city's central and Near South Side. By 1847, there were enough Black people in Chicago to organize the city's first Black congregation at Quinn Chapel African Methodist Episcopal Church, which was located at Jackson and Dearborn before its original location was destroyed in the Great Chicago Fire of 1871.

1850

The Fugitive Slave Act, passed in 1850, made law officials responsible for capturing and returning freedom seekers, even in free states. Black people fled to Canada.

1853

The Illinois General Assembly passed then-state Rep. John Logan's Black Law of 1853, which prohibited Black folks from settling in Illinois and further encouraged the exodus of Black Illinoisans. Today, Chicago's Logan Square neighborhood is named after him.

1865

Illinois repealed the Black Law in January 1865, and became the first state to ratify the 13th Amendment, which abolished slavery. New relatively liberating rights were being granted to Black people while the U.S. government was still robbing Indigenous people of their land. The Civil Rights Act of 1866 declared that Indigenous tribes couldn't claim U.S. citizenship, which gave Uncle Sam more leeway to do grimy things like strong-arm them into unfavorable treaties.

1870

In Chicago, and across the U.S., 1870 marked the first time Black men were able to vote, with the ratification of the 15th Amendment.

10 LIKELY
SL
AT
On THURS
WE
In front of our Office, wit
AT
10 AS LIK
As any ever offered in this superior Cook and House first rate House Servant, a

Wednesday, July 23, 1823.

1893 PAINTING THE "WHITE CITY" BLACK

In 1893, Chicago hosted a grand exhibition of American culture, industry, scholarship and technological advancements. The World's Columbian Exposition was a world's fair, with 46 participating countries. From May 1 to Oct. 30, the city attracted more than 27 million visitors to its fairgrounds in Jackson Park. Fairgoers endearingly dubbed it the "White City," because of the striking white color of the artificial stone, called "staff," typically used for temporary buildings. Black people called it "White City," too, but for a different reason.

Black people weren't allowed to participate in the process of organizing the World's Columbian Exposition. Since all exhibits had to be approved by a committee of white men, Black exhibits were few and far between. However, Black Americans weren't going to be shut out of a celebration of American progress that had been driven by their labor. The World's Columbian Exposition was a chance to reclaim their narrative on a global stage.

The only participating Black country, Haiti, welcomed Black folk to use their building as a platform for protest. The Haitian government appointed abolitionist Frederick Douglass (a.k.a "The most famous Black man in America") as their representative at the World's Columbian Exposition. The fair also brought famed muckraking journalist Ida B. Wells to Chicago on her worldwide anti-lynching tour.

Wells collaborated with Douglass, journalist Irvine Garland Penn, and founder of the *Chicago Conservator* Ferdinand Lee Barnett to publish a pamphlet called "The Reason Why the Colored American Is Not in the World's Columbian Exposition," explaining how they lobbied for a seat at the table but were denied. Their pamphlet was distributed to at least 10,000 people.

Haiti Building at the World's Columbian Exposition, Chicago, Illinois, 1893.

VALUABLE
VES
TION.

he 24th inst.

E! 2,

of ~~mit~~ or reserve for cash,

JK,

NEGROES

ong them is a man who is a
 girl about 17 years old, a
~~t~~ seamstress.

KE & HUBBARD,
Auctioneers.

Broadside advertising a slave auction outside of Brooke and Hubbard Auctioneers office, Richmond, Virginia, July 23, 1823.

1871

The Great Chicago Fire of 1871 is credited as the turning point for the city's development into a modern metropolis. However, another seldom-mentioned fire happened a few years later in 1874 that devastated the city's Black community in the South Loop area.

1872

During the 1870s, Black Chicagoans set their eyes on politics and other positions of power in the city. Soon to follow, James L. Shelton became the first Black Chicago policeman in 1871. The Chicago Fire Department saw its first Black fire company, Engine Company 21, in 1872. John W. E. Thomas became the first Black legislator elected to the Illinois General Assembly in 1876.

1878

Ferdinand Lee Barnett, a lawyer, journalist, and Reconstruction era civil rights activist, founded the *Chicago Conservator*, the city's first Black publication, in 1878. He became only the third Black person to pass to the Illinois Bar.

View of the corner of State and Madison Streets after the Chicago Fire of 1871, Chicago, Illinois.

1917

An Illinois court dismissed a complaint by the Pokagon band of Potawatami, who fought to reclaim unceded land that had become Lake Shore Drive. The complaint went to the Supreme Court in 1917, where the judge didn't see a need to determine the original rights of submerged lands.

GERTIE BROWN

An actress and vaudeville performer born in Ohio in 1878, Brown was a part of the Rag-Time Four performers. She performed in vaudeville and minstrel shows in Chicago. She was also a regular performer at the Pekin Theatre. In 2017, a film clip was discovered from the silent film "Something Good - Negro Kiss," which featured Brown and co-star Saint Suttle kissing passionately. It was filmed in Chicago in 1898. It is said to be the first example of on-screen intimacy between two Black people. The film was added to the Library of Congress' National Film Registry in 2018.

Lincoln Perry, the actor and comedian known as Stepin Fetchit, poses in Los Angeles before boarding a flight to the 1927 NAACP benefit in New York.

FOSTER PHOTOPLAY COMPANY

The nation's first Black film production company was founded in Chicago in 1910 by William Foster, a newspaperman, vaudeville press agent, and theatrical manager. He moved to Chicago and soon became the Pekin Theatre's business rep. Foster had a desire to show the depth and humanity of Black people in film, something that was missing in films by white filmmakers. He debuted his first short, a two-reel comedy called "The Railroad Porter," in 1912.

LINCOLN PERRY

An actor and tap dancer best known for his controversial role as Stepin Fetchit, he was the first Black movie star and the first Black performer to be named in a movie's credits and given a studio contract with Fox Film Corporation. He also has a star on the Hollywood Walk of Fame under the name Stepin Fetchit. Perry was an entertainment critic for the *Chicago Defender*. His column was first called "Lincoln Perry Writes" and was later renamed "Lincoln Perry's Letter." Perry achieved significant success in film and got his big break in 1927 in the silent film, "In Old Kentucky." He lived in public housing in the 1970s, and his neighbors asked the Chicago Housing Authority to name the building after him. In 1979, the Bronzeville housing project became the Lincoln Perry Apartments.

LIGHTS, CAMERA, ACTION!

HOW BLACK HOLLYWOOD GOT ITS START IN CHICAGO

By Tonia Hill

At a time when minstrel shows were all the buzz and there were limited opportunities for Black people in the theater scene, Chicago's film and theater industry pioneers found ways to portray Black life outside of the stereotypical minstrel caricatures.

Originally published in summer 2021

THE PEKIN THEATRE

a.k.a., the "temple of music," was founded in 1905 by saloon owner and policy king Robert T. Motts. It was the first Black-owned theater in Chicago and one of the first to feature Black performers. The Pekin was one of few venues for entertainment available to Black people in Chicago. It was the place to see jazz, theater, and vaudeville acts. Successful shows at the Pekin include "The Man from 'Bam," "The Mayor of Dixie," and "The Husband." Motts ran Pekin until he died in 1911.

Oscar Micheaux Presents The Gunsaulus Mystery
WITH
EVELYN PREER —
— DICK ABRAMS
L. DE BULGER —
LAWRENCE CHENAULT
and a notable supporting colored cast

A lobby card for the 1921 silent film "The Gunsaulus Mystery." The poster features Oscar Micheaux who was the writer and director of the film.

OSCAR MICHEAUX

A film pioneer, independent filmmaker, producer, and director who has more than 40 feature films under his belt, he worked as a Pullman Porter before starting his film career. He also worked in Chicago stockyards and steel mills. His first feature, "The Homesteader," debuted in 1919. He was inspired by Chicago's Black Metropolis and in his films, he showed Black people as fully human — a pivot from how Black people were portrayed in films by white filmmakers at the time.

of Mary Richardson Jones, taken
ne after 1883

can journalist and civil rights
st, Ida B. Wells, 1920

BLACK WOMEN'S SUFFRAGE MOVEMENT IN ILLINOIS

By Kelly Garcia

Originally published in summer 2021

We can't talk about abolition today without talking about the Black women integral to the movement. In Chicago, Ida B. Wells was essential to building political power for Black women. As an investigative journalist, teacher, anti-lynching crusader and mother, Wells was already influential to the national political arena before making an impression on Chicago politics.

Before Wells' arrival near the turn of the twentieth century, Black people in the Chicago area and across Illinois were already engaged in a long fight to abolish slavery and end racial discrimination. In 1871, Chicagoan John Jones became the first Black elected official in Illinois. Jones led the charge to repeal the Black Codes, a set of discriminatory laws against Black people.

Along with his wife Mary Richardson Jones, the Joneses were crucial to the abolition of slavery and emancipation. Richardson Jones helped found a club dedicated to Black political action and directing aid to former enslaved people, called the Chicago Colored Ladies Freedmen's Aid Society. Together, she and her husband opened their doors to freedom seeker making their way north on the Underground Railroad and created a space for abolitionists to meet and organize.

After John Jones' passing in 1879, his estate —left to his wife— was worth more than $70,000 (that's $1.8 million in 2021). She contributed to the Hull House, the Phyllis Wheatley Club and Provident Hospital, while also dedicating herself to the suffrage movement, becoming one of the first Black women to lead the fight before her passing in 1910.

By that point, the women's suffrage movement had gained momentum, but also garnered criticism for excluding Black women. In 1896, Wells helped establish the National Association of Colored Women's Clubs (NACWC), a merger of several organizations advocating for Black women's suffrage and civil rights. The NACWC opened the doors for many Black women leaders, including Chicagoan Dr. Mary Fitzbutler Waring, who later became NACWC's 10th president during the Great Depression in the 1930s.

As president, Waring raised awareness on anti-lynching bills and worked tirelessly to make segregation illegal. She was also known for her leadership in the medical profession and paving the way for more Black female physicians. The NACWC went on to become one of the most influential organizations for Black women's suffrage and has since continued to pave the way for community service and activism.

Aside from the NACWC, Wells also created the first and one of the most important organizations dedicated to Black women's suffrage in Illinois: the Alpha Suffrage Club. Her goal was to expand the women's suffrage movement to include Black women and to build their political power. She was widely criticized by other leaders of the larger women's suffrage movement whose primary intent was to win voting rights for white women only.

Wells was keen on expanding Black women's suffrage nationally, and in 1914 she tapped Chicagoan Mary C. Byron to create a suffrage organization for Black women in Missouri. Byron was also a member of Negro Women's Civic League in Chicago's Sixth Ward, focusing on the political struggles of Black women in Chicago. In 1914, Oscar De Priest was elected as the first Black alderman of Chicago's City Council, a feat largely attributed to the Alpha Suffrage Club.

Byron went on to leave a long-lasting impression in Illinois politics, later becoming the first Black woman to run for a seat in the Illinois General Assembly. Her platform included a standard wage for domestic workers, protection of women in industry work, and a state school board. Despite losing her election, Byron continued to run for office including once for Cook County Commissioner, but unfortunately never won a seat.

How the Chicago Fire of 1874 and the World's Columbian Exposition of 1893 Led to the Formation of the Black Belt

By Tonia Hill

Originally published in summer 2021

The notion that Black life in Chicago began during the first wave of the Great Migration in the 1910s isn't accurate. Black Chicago's origin story began when Chicago's first non-Indigenous settler, a Black man named Jean Baptiste Pointe DuSable, came and set down roots in the 1780s.

While the bulk of Black folks arrived in the 20th century, there was a small, yet thriving Black community near what we now refer to as the South Loop. Some of those "old settlers" include abolitionists John and Mary Jane Richardson-Jones, Joseph and Anna Elizabeth Hudlin—the first Black people to own and build their own home in Chicago—and politician John W. E. Thomas.

However, on a scorching hot summer day in July of 1874, Chicago experienced its second major fire in three years. On July 14, the fire started near the northeast corner of Clark and 12th Street (now Roosevelt), less than a mile east of where the Great Chicago Fire of 1871 started on Dekoven and Jefferson Streets. Over the span of eight hours, the fire burned more than 47 acres, destroying more than 800 buildings and killing 20 people. Eighty-five percent of Black-owned property in the city burned, including John and Mary Jane Richardson-Jones' home, according to Dempsey Travis' book *An Autobiography of Black Chicago*.

In 1870, there were more than 3,600 Black people in Chicago, and the population grew to more than 14,000 by 1890, according to Dr. Christopher Robert Reed's book, *Black Chicago's First Century, Volume I: 1833-1900*. The 1874 fire became known as the Second Chicago Fire. Coupled with the World's Columbian Exposition of 1893, it shaped the trajectory of Black Chicago through the formation of the Black Belt and the population growth that followed.

"You start seeing the dispersal of these African Americans further south, and to the west, and that's one of the first ways that we see some of the racialized enclaves that we would come to know later begin to form," said Julius Jones, an assistant curator at the Chicago History Museum. Jones developed an exhibit, "City on Fire," which opened in October 2021, which was the 150th anniversary of the 1871 fire.

DISPLACEMENT AFTER THE FIRE

The area devastated by the 1874 fire was mostly inhabited by Jewish immigrants and middle-class Black people. According to Jones, both communities lived in relative peace and harmony before the fire. At the same time, white people viewed the area as impoverished and vice-ridden. The loss of Black property during the fire was a blessing to white real-estate speculators — after all, it was close to the lake. After the fire, Jewish immigrants moved further west and north into neighborhoods such as the Near West Side, Lawndale and Albany Park. Black people moved farther south, forming what would later become Bronzeville.

As Black Chicagoans moved south, they landed between 12th and 79th Streets and Cottage Grove and Wentworth Avenues. According to Lee Bey, a Chicago native and adjunct professor of architecture at the Illinois Institute of Technology, Black folks were confined to the Black Belt by design after the first and second waves of the Great Migration.

The architects of the Black Belt were state and local officials who created and practiced racist and discriminatory policies to limit the movement of Black people in the city, including restrictive covenants that barred Black people from buying or renting property in majority-white neighborhoods.

Black Chicago's most prized cultural institutions — such as the Regal Theater, the Sunset Café, the DuSable Museum of African American History, and others — were formed in the Black Belt during the first half of the 20th century. This area was also home to Black Chicago's literary greats Lorraine Hansberry, Gwendolyn Brooks and many others. Powerful Black business corridors were also established in neighborhoods such as Chatham.

"By creating a city within a city, because we couldn't live anyplace else, we couldn't shop for the most part anyplace else. If we work someplace else, when that shift was over, we better get back to where we 'belonged.' You know, [racism] triggers what it always triggers with Black people, which is how we're going to use self-reliance to remove the sting of this," Bey said. "So, as a result, we had our own stores, entertainment, everything that a city would have."

DEMANDING RESPECT AT THE WORLD'S FAIR

All eyes turned to Chicago while it hosted the World's Fair in 1893 in Jackson Park. During its six-month run, more than 27 million people visited the fairgrounds at Jackson Park. The fairgoers included many current and future Black Chicago leaders such as Robert S. Abbott, future founder of the Chicago Defender.

Bey also credits Abbott as an architect of the Black Belt. Abbott performed at the fairgrounds with a quartet from Hampton University. He loved what he saw so much during that trip that he made Chicago his permanent home in 1897.

Through the *Defender*, Abbott encouraged Black people to flee from the racial terror of the South to the North, where there was more economic opportunity available to them.

"The calls to come from the South, to come to work in the factories, comes from Robert Abbott, who basically puts the call out in the newspaper, and the newspaper flows down south on trains through Pullman Porters, that basically is saying, 'Come off that plow,'" Bey said. "'Come out of that degradation that you're going through, and come here.'"

Although the fire of 1874 and the 1893 World Columbian Exposition had their fair share of positive outcomes for the Black community at the time, both moments stand as precursors to what Black people in Chicago still experience today.

"When you talk about 85% of homes owned by African Americans being destroyed in the fire, we're talking about the loss of having that asset that will appreciate and thus help you build wealth," Jones said. "You see that time and time again [in the Black community]; the inability to build wealth due to hardship, disaster, race, racialized and racist policies."

African American janitors of the Columbian Guard at the World's Columbian Exposition, Chicago, Illinois, 1893

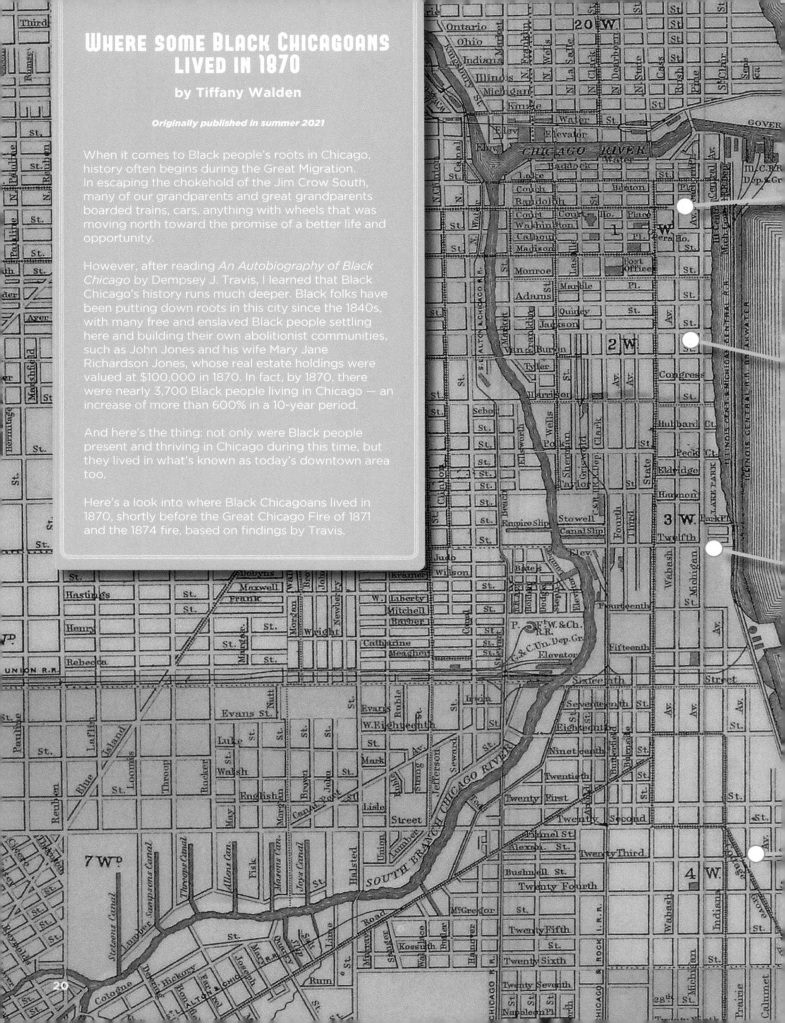

Where some Black Chicagoans lived in 1870

by Tiffany Walden

Originally published in summer 2021

When it comes to Black people's roots in Chicago, history often begins during the Great Migration. In escaping the chokehold of the Jim Crow South, many of our grandparents and great grandparents boarded trains, cars, anything with wheels that was moving north toward the promise of a better life and opportunity.

However, after reading *An Autobiography of Black Chicago* by Dempsey J. Travis, I learned that Black Chicago's history runs much deeper. Black folks have been putting down roots in this city since the 1840s, with many free and enslaved Black people settling here and building their own abolitionist communities, such as John Jones and his wife Mary Jane Richardson Jones, whose real estate holdings were valued at $100,000 in 1870. In fact, by 1870, there were nearly 3,700 Black people living in Chicago — an increase of more than 600% in a 10-year period.

And here's the thing: not only were Black people present and thriving in Chicago during this time, but they lived in what's known as today's downtown area too.

Here's a look into where Black Chicagoans lived in 1870, shortly before the Great Chicago Fire of 1871 and the 1874 fire, based on findings by Travis.

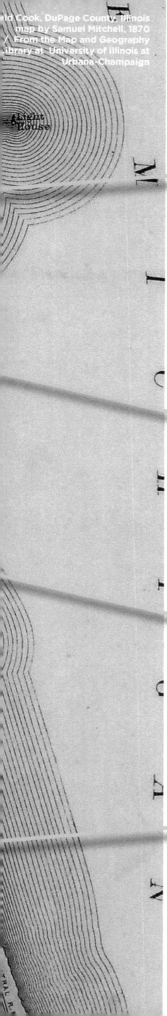

NEGRO PROPERTY OWNERS IN CHICAGO IN 1870

WARD 1

- **Name: Robert Chatman** | Age: 22 | Property location: 365 Wells | Old occupation: Porter | New occupation: Waiter | Value of real estate: $700

- **Name: John Holmes** | Age: 40 | Property location: 209 Market | Old occupation: Whitewasher | New occupation: Same | Value of real estate: $3,000

- **Name: Stephen Stamps** | Age: 42 | Property location: 183 Monroe Old occupation: Saloon keeper | New occupation: Same | Value of real estate: $20,000

WARD 2

- **Name: George Alexander** | Age: 40 | Property location: Loomis Street Old occupation: Porter | New occupation: Janitor | Value of real estate: $6,000

- **Name: Oliver J. Jacobs** | Age: 35 | Property location: 88 4th Avenue Old occupation: Carpenter | New occupation:Restaurateur | Value of real estate: $10,000

- **Name: John Jone**s | Age: 54 | Property location: 218 Edina Place Old occupation: Tailor | New occupation: Same | Value of real estate: $100,000

WARD 3

- **Charles Anderson** | Age: 40 | Property location: 331 State Street Old occupation: Church sexton | New occupation: Same | Value of real estate: $700

- **Adelaida Jackson** | Age: 49 | Property location: 72 Quincy Old occupation: Housekeeper | New occupation: Same | Value of real estate: $2,000

- **Henry Moore** | Age: 46 | Property location: 196 4th Avenue | Old occupation: Laborer | New occupation: Porter | Value of real estate: $3,000

WARD 4

- **Name: Frank Boone** | Age: 68 | Property location: 365 State Street | Old occupation: Teamster | New occupation: Room Tender | Value of real estate: $1,000

- **Name: George W. Browne** | Age: 35 | Property location: 129 4th Avenue Old occupation: Carpenter/Builder | New occupation: Same | Value of real estate: $7,000

- **Name: John Young** | Age: 30 | Property location: 363 Clark Street Old occupation: Mailer/Cook | New occupation: Same | Value of real estate: $5,400

Source: 1870 U.S. Census Report, and City of Chicago Directory, 1870

Portrait of Mary Richardson Jones, circa 1865

Portrait of John Jones, circa 1865

The Rise of Black Political Power in Early Chicago

By Arionne Nettles   *Originally published in summer 2021*

When John and Mary Jane Richardson Jones settled in Chicago in 1845, it was just seven decades after Jean Baptiste Pointe DuSable became the city's first non-Indigenous settler.

With only $3 in their possession, the couple moved from downstate Alton, Ill., with their baby and soon built wealth in the burgeoning city. John Jones opened a tailor shop on Dearborn Street between Harrison and Polk streets, becoming one of the wealthiest Black men in the United States, with a fortune valued at up to $100,000 (worth $3.2 million in 2021).

When Dr. Bruce Purnell, a descendent of the Joneses and the executive director of The Love-More Movement, Inc., first learned about his family's story, he was 19 years old. As he looked through the family documents and photos passed down to him, the story of John and Mary Jane Richardson Jones became more and more surreal.

"I'm still processing it really," said Purnell, who is 53 years old. "The fact that he was a station master for the Underground Railroad and an organizer of the Civil War and assistant pallbearer in [President Abraham] Lincoln's funeral. Wow, I didn't know any of this. Putting it together, I actually got to see the story, like, oh. This is real. This is who he is."

From the 1840s to the 1860s, the Joneses used their influence to fight against the Illinois Black Codes that prohibited Black people from voting, required them to

in the state, and even denied them the right to gather in groups of three or more without the risk of being jailed or beaten.

Even in the city's earliest days, Black people in Chicago helped create the city we know today. From abolition to the fight for political office, their work helped to establish

But during the time of slavery, this political power looked different — it took on the form of abolition and protection.

Quinn Chapel, an A.M.E. church then located at State and Madison in the heart of the city, served as a station on the Underground Railroad. Chicago was often one of the last stops before Detroit and Canada.

"Once the church got started, one of the first ministries of the church was a vigilance society where men of the community got together to patrol, to make sure that folks weren't getting snatched up and taken back into slavery had they escaped, or free people without their papers being snatched up [illegally]," said Will Miller, Quinn Chapel's historic preservation chair.

At the time, Black people had to carry certificates of freedom that said they were free. In 1850, the Fugitive Slave Act denied enslaved people a right to trial by jury and required citizens in the state to help in apprehending them. And in 1853, Illinois responded to the Fugitive Slave Act by prohibiting all Black people from entering the state.

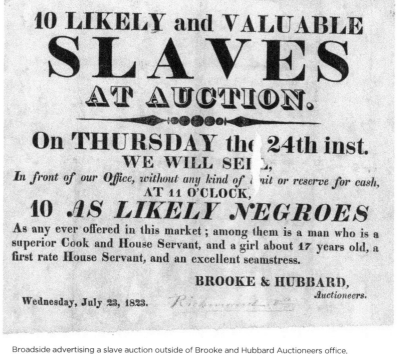

10 LIKELY and VALUABLE SLAVES AT AUCTION.

On THURSDAY the 24th inst. WE WILL SELL, In front of our Office, without any kind of limit or reserve for cash, AT 11 O'CLOCK, 10 AS LIKELY NEGROES As any ever offered in this market; among them is a man who is a superior Cook and House Servant, and a girl about 17 years old, a first rate House Servant, and an excellent seamstress.

BROOKE & HUBBARD, Auctioneers.

Wednesday, July 23, 1823.

Broadside advertising a slave auction outside of Brooke and Hubbard Auctioneers office, Richmond, Virginia, July 23, 1823.

But even with their privilege and wealth, the Joneses still were not safe in Chicago.

"If a free Black person in Chicago, [even] someone of John and Mary Jane Jones' stature, didn't have the freedom papers with them on any given day, it could be disastrous for them," said John Russick, senior vice president of the Chicago History Museum.

After the Civil War ended in 1865, more Black people migrated to Chicago and their population reached nearly 4,000 people in 1870, exponentially rising to 15,000 by 1890. Before Black men received the legal right to vote in 1870, and the passing of local anti-discrimination laws in the Illinois Civil Rights Act of 1885, Black people expanded their power by collaborating with white politicians, explained Claire Hartfield, educator and author of *A Few Red Drops: The Chicago Race Riot of 1919*.

"Black leaders put in a ton of time and strategy behind the scenes collecting petitions and talking to people around the state, to try to get a groundswell to get rid of those kinds of laws," Hartfield said. "They did all the work — they didn't get the credit."

" I THINK THE THING THAT OFTEN GETS OVERLOOKED WITH COMMUNITIES WHO ARE ON THE MARGINS OF POLITICAL POWER IS THAT IT'S NOT THAT THEY DON'T HAVE ANY POLITICAL POWER. THEY HAVE INFLUENCE.

At Quinn, a group of Black women abolitionists who worked at the church were referred to as "The Big Four," and Mary Jane Richardson Jones was one of them. The daughter of a free Black blacksmith, she married John Jones in 1841. He was the son of a free mixed woman and a German man, and had fled his home state of North Carolina because his mother feared his father would enslave him.

In 1898, Archibald Carey Sr. became pastor of Quinn Chapel. He campaigned for the Republican Party and got close with William Thompson, who would eventually become Chicago's mayor in 1915. Through his relationships, Carey later became the city's chief examiner of claims and a civil service commissioner, where he made sure the city hired more Black police and punished officers who unfairly treated Black people.

"I think the thing that often gets overlooked with communities who are on the margins of political power is that it's not that they don't have any political power. They have influence," Russick said. "With real population growth comes real political power, and when you see someone like John Jones have influence, [it's] because, in part, he's a successful businessman, he does hold elected office in Chicago and he is part of a movement to change America's relationship with enslaved people."

"AS WE TALK ABOUT TELLING OUR OWN STORY AND CHANGING THE NARRATIVE, WHERE'S THE FOUNDATION OF THAT? THE FOUNDATION CAN'T COME THROUGH OUR OPPRESSOR AS WE TELL OUR STORY,"

In the 1910s, Black political power continued to grow with the expansion of women's voting rights. "Just like today, Black women carried things on their back," Hartfield said.

In 1913, Illinois women gained limited suffrage to vote for president and in some local elections. The famed Ida B. Wells took advantage of that opportunity by encouraging Black women to use their voting power. She had created the Alpha Suffrage Club earlier that year, and the group used a grassroots approach in knocking on doors and getting Black women registered to vote. Wells attributes their effort to getting Oscar Stanton De Priest, Chicago's first Black alderman, elected to the City Council in 1914.

"The women who joined were extremely interested when I showed them that we could use our vote for the advantage of ourselves and our race," Wells wrote in her autobiography, Crusade for Justice.

Black trailblazers in Chicago paved the way for the country to see its first Black president, and this political power was established as the city's Black community was still growing — long before the Great Migration started in 1916 and before Chicago's Black population would double before 1940. Yet, this legacy of Black political activism and organizing is often unknown and is something Purnell, the descendant of the Joneses, said should be our current foundation, especially as he looks toward the future and to those who will continue to build his family's legacy.

"As we talk about telling our own story and changing the narrative, where's the foundation of that? The foundation can't come through our oppressor as we tell our story," Purnell said. "I want [my grandson] to know who he is and that this is about liberation."

Portrait of Oscar Stanton De Priest, 1915.

Louis Armstrong at the Sutherland Hotel, 4659 South Drexel Boulevard, Chicago,

BLACK METROPOLIS
1901 - 1960

Joe Louis and his wife at the Bud Billiken Day parade, Chicago, Illinois, August 9, 1948.

View of a crowd celebrating the James Braddock vs. Joe Louis boxing match at the Sunset Café

III: BLACK METROPOLIS
(1901-1960)
by Matt Harvey

By 1910, Chicago's Black population had reached more than 40,000, while the city's Indigenous population had declined significantly. Once the first wave of the Great Migration from the South kicked off, another 50,000 Black folks settled on the South and Near West sides of the city between 1916 and 1920. In Chicago, the absence of de jure segregation (meaning there weren't laws enforcing segregation), meant more economic mobility and freedom to thrive.

And if the 1920s were roaring anywhere in the country, they were certainly roaring in Chicago's Bronzeville neighborhood. The list of iconic Black artists who thrived in Bronzeville during Chicago's Black Renaissance include Louis Armstrong, Bessie Coleman, Langston Hughes, Katherine Dunham, Richard Wright and more. The South Side community boasted a Black population of more than 300,000 at its peak in 1952, according to poet Gwendolyn Brooks in a Holiday Magazine article.

With the establishment of vital Black-run institutions in the city, it quickly grew into a Black metropolis, which actually became its nickname. After World War II, another wave of Black and Indigenous people came to Chicago, many to work factory jobs that were now being offered to them in the booming post-war industry.

Between the 1940s and 1960s, the federal government terminated sovereignty for Indigenous groups, purchasing one-way bus tickets to relocate them to urban centers such as Chicago, where the government hoped they would assimilate and become another indistinguishable group.

1908

Because Black Chicagoans still experienced discrimination in the financial world, Jesse Binga founded the first privately-owned Black bank in the city in 1908. He later expanded with a state charter, opening The Binga State Bank in 1921.

1933

The National De Saible Memorial Society, under the leadership of Black educator and culturist Annie Oliver, succeeded in getting its replica of the home of Jean Pointe Baptiste DuSable exhibited at the 1933 Chicago World's Fair. Up until the De Saible Memorial Society's pamphlet and exhibit, most Chicagoans had never heard of DuSable, and many visitors to the fair were shocked to learn that the city — that was then being celebrated as one of the greatest in the world — was first settled by a Black man.

1919

Georgia Blues musician Thomas Andrew Dorsey moved to Chicago in 1919. At the time, Black churches mostly condemned Blues music for its "sinful" themes, according to PBS. Imagine a Black church without clapping and stomping, without the rhythmic drumming and organs — that's what it was like before Dorsey came through and shook things up. Dorsey is remembered as the Father of Gospel Music.

On July 27, 17-year-old Eugene Williams was stoned by a white mob while swimming at 29th Street beach for having drifted too far north into an imaginary racial line. Williams drowned, and police refused to arrest the white man responsible. This was the tipping point for a city boiling with racial tensions. Riots began at the beach and spread throughout the Black Belt on the South Side. White mobs attacked Black residents with stones and looted their homes. The riot lasted seven days, and cost the lives of 15 white and 23 Black people. More than 537 more people — a majority of them Black — were injured.

1932

In 1932, the Hall branch of the Chicago Public Library (CPL) was built in Bronzeville and run by Vivian Harsh, the first Black librarian in the history of the CPL. The branch was named after Dr. George Cleveland Hall, a former Provident Hospital chief of staff, civic leader and CPL board member who fought to have the branch created. Harsh hosted the Book Review and Lecture Forum (BRLF) at Hall branch, which featured speakers such as Zora Neale Hurston, Langston Hughes, Gwendolyn Brooks, Margaret Walker and Richard Wright — all discussing Black history, literature and current events. These writers and more contributed to the Special Negro Collection, an archive of Black literature that is Harsh's crowning achievement.

Gwendolyn Brooks, a Pulitzer Prize in Poetry winner for "Annie Allen," a ballad of Chicago Negro life. The first woman to capture one of the famed awards.

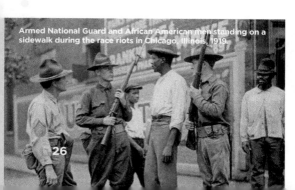

Armed National Guard and African American men standing on a sidewalk during the race riots in Chicago, Illinois, 1919.

1949 Displacement for Expressways 1953

These days, the Dan Ryan and the 290 Expressways are known to most Chicagoans as the easiest ways to go to and from out South or out West, respectively. But looking back at the 1940s and 1950s, the two expressways have dark pasts. Both functioned as tools for segregation and the displacement of Black Chicagoans.

In 1949, wrecking crews pulled up to the Near West Side—which had the highest proportion of Black residents in the city at the time—and started tearing things down to make way for the Eisenhower Expressway, a.k.a. I-290. Businesses, factories and homes were all destroyed to make way for the incoming roadway. The destruction was encouraged by some white residents who celebrated the removal of Black slums. Under the protection of eminent domain laws — which allow the government to claim ownership of private land in order to convert it for public use — there was nothing residents of the area could do to fight it. They were forced to move further west to predominantly white immigrant areas such as East Garfield Park and Humboldt Park — places where they were far from safe.

Meanwhile, the city was pulling the same trick out South with the construction of the Dan Ryan Expressway. The original plans for the expressway had it cutting through the predominantly white immigrant community of Bridgeport, where then-Mayor Richard J. Daley and his family lived. Daley opted to move the construction a little further east to Wentworth, and commandeered properties in the predominantly Black area for the construction. This move forced Black Southsiders into smaller areas and housing projects such as Stateway Gardens and the Robert Taylor Homes, which were constructed next to the Dan Ryan to handle the overcrowding of slums.

Slowly, the Native American community grew in Chicago because of the Indian Termination Policy, which dismantled tribal sovereignty. The American Indian Center was founded in 1953 to support those who left their homes on the reservation. Located in Uptown, it later became a relocation center after the Indian Relocation Act of 1956 as the Native American population grew from about 500 to 10,000 between 1945 and 1975, according to historian James B. LaGrand's 2002 book "Indian Metropolis: Native Americans in Chicago, 1945-75."

1940

In 1940, a group of local artists called the Arts and Crafts Guild (Charles White, Bernard Goss, George Neal, Eldzier Cortor, Gordon Parks, Archibald Motley and Margaret Taylor-Burroughs) raised enough money — with the help of local residents, business people, and art collectors — to purchase a large house in Bronzeville that would become home to the South Side Community Art Center. The South Side Community Art Center, located at 3831 S. Michigan, is the first Black art institution in the United States.

Advertisement poster for the American Negro Exposition at the Chicago Coliseum, Chicago, Illinois.

American Negro Exposition

After limited inclusion in the 1933 Chicago World's Fair, Black people were fed up. In the early 20th century, Black people had made many major contributions to American industries. So they decided to take matters into their own hands.

In 1934, real estate businessman James Washington began lobbying for funding for an exposition highlighting Black accomplishments. Washington spent five years securing endorsements and money for his "Afra-Merican Emancipation Exposition," one that would commemorate the 75th anniversary of emancipation in 1940.

On July 4, 1940, the American Negro Exposition opened at the Chicago Coliseum at Wabash Avenue and 15th Street.

Of the more than 120 exhibits included, one was the Court of Dioramas highlighting historical events such as Ethiopians using the first wheel and Arctic explorer Matthew Henson's journey to the North Pole. Tanner Hall, in another wing of the Coliseum, was described as the "greatest collection of Negro art ever assembled." Black creatives including Langston Hughes, Paul Robeson and Duke Ellington participated in the exhibition, which was a national phenomenon.

Less than four months after the exposition closed in September 1940, despite the financial support of the government and appearance of Chicago Mayor Edward Kelly and President Franklin Delano Roosevelt, it was back to business as usual in regards to Chicago's racist aggressions toward its Black citizens. A restrictive covenant went into effect that made it illegal for anyone with at least ⅛ Negro blood to live in the area around the Coliseum.

THE CHICAGO BLACK RENAISSANCE IS HARLEM'S RADICAL COUNTERPART

By Crystal Hill

Originally published in summer 2021

In the wake of the Harlem Renaissance — a culturally renowned period of Black excellence in the 1920s — a lesser-known, but equally powerful movement emerged in Chicago.

As Harlem's movement lost steam in the 1930s, a number of Black Chicagoans — many of them young, working-class and residing on the South Side — wrote poems, authored novels and created paintings and sculptures that reflected sharply leftist socioeconomic views, as well as the scrappy, urban industrial culture of the city in a manner that historians say distinguished it from Harlem.

"Beginning in the 1930s and lasting into the 1950s, [Black] Chicago experienced a cultural renaissance that rivaled, and some argue, exceeded the cultural outpouring in Harlem," writes Darlene Clark Hine, the John A. Hannah Distinguished Professor at Michigan State University's Department of History. She is a prominent scholar of African-American history and co-author of *The Black Chicago Renaissance*.

"The Black Chicago Renaissance, however," Hine wrote, "has yet to receive its full due."

The awakening in Chicago was borne out of Bronzeville, a historically Black neighborhood known as the Black Metropolis, where many artists, musicians and writers resided. Similarly, Harlem was home to Black residents with limited housing options who had come from the South during the Great Migration. There was some overlap between both movements, with Harlem-era artists like Arna Bontemps relocating to Chicago, and acclaimed poet Langston Hughes becoming a columnist at the *Chicago Defender* after the Harlem Renaissance.

But despite introducing the world to celebrated artists such as author Richard Wright (best known for his novel Native Son and memoir Black Boy) and Pulitzer Prize-winning poet Gwendolyn Brooks (the first Black writer to win the Pulitzer), the Chicago Black Renaissance still seems to lag behind the Harlem movement in terms of clout and recognition — even as scholars say the Chicago revival's impact is undeniable.

"It was impactful in terms of art production," Erik Gellman, a history professor at the University of North Carolina at Chapel Hill, told *The TRiiBE*. "But it was also impactful in terms of creating art for political purposes that connected strongly with social protest movements of the 1930s and 1940s. So it sort of helped create a kind of working-class militant Black counterculture that mattered beyond the art world itself."

Mahalia Jackson singing at home with Thomas A Dorsey accompanying on the piano, Chicago, Illinois circa 1960

South Side Community Art Center's Black Expressions Art winners nounced, 3831 South Michigan Avenue, Chicago, Illinois.

The Harlem movement stemmed in part from the belief that exhibiting intellectual and artistic excellence would lead to the advancement of Black people in America, although both movements centered the Black experience, according to the late Samuel Floyd Jr., a Chicago scholar who founded the Center for Black Music Research at Columbia College. Floyd wrote an article in the *Black Chicago Renaissance*, stating that the art in New York City was often supported by "wealthy [Black] and white philanthropists, publishers, entrepreneurs, and socialists who wanted to promote the aesthetic advancement of the race."

The Black Chicago Renaissance, However, has yet to receive its full due."

In a 2012 column for the *Chicago Tribune*, then-columnist Dawn Turner Trice wrote that "unlike the Harlem Renaissance, the Chicago movement didn't have as its face such well-known intellectuals as W.E.B. Du Bois." She adds that "Chicago artists didn't have relatively large numbers of wealthy white patrons who helped support their art."

"The Harlem Renaissance is often taught as a group of artists who removed themselves from the larger urban scene to collectively produce all of this work, and their work [was] often the product of collaboration with white entrepreneurs or benefactors," Gellman said. As a result, they "weren't that invested in the politics and the currents of what was happening in the larger community."

Archival photos courtesy of the Chicago History Museum

The Harlem Renaissance happened in an era "wrapped up in the politics of respectability, sort of striving for the 'Talented Tenth' kind of idea," Gellman said. Chicago was different.

"It was public. It was working class. Anyone could participate," he said of Chicago's renaissance. "And it was a very public-facing endeavor that was oriented towards working-class people, ordinary people. Rather than saying, 'we are artists, we need to detach ourselves from the society we're in,' [Chicago's artists] actually engaged with the society they were in and engaged in the kind of radical politics of their day. And that informed their artwork."

This included artists such as Charles Wright, a Chicago painter whose work featured Black men doing manual labor during a time when Black Chicagoans worked strenuous jobs for low wages in factories and rail yards, experiencing economic disparities steeped in racism.

"These artists were greatly influenced by Marxism," Dr. Kelli Morgan, an art scholar and curator, said in a Youtube video, "and the role of the Black worker in American society was very important to their work."

She added that through the image of the Black worker, artists like Wright aimed to "critique the power structures behind these conditions." It wasn't uncommon for Black artists and intellectuals to engage in radical leftist politics tied to Marxism and the Communist Party, according to Hine.

Artists such as poet and painter Margaret Burroughs were exceptional

creators and intellectuals, "but they were also very working class people," Gellman said. "They made art, not to be hung in a gallery or bought by a white patron, but to be shown or [displayed] in the South Side Community Art Center, or to be exhibited at the YMCA. It was art for a different purpose and a different audience."

The working-class ethos of Chicago's movement may play a role in how it's perceived decades later and whether it has a place in today's classrooms. In July 2012, dozens of high school teachers from across the country came to Chicago to participate in a program on the Black Chicago Renaissance, with the intention of learning about the renaissance and incorporating that knowledge into their curriculum, according to Gellman and NPR station WBEZ.

Gellman believes that a high school teacher is likely to find the Harlem Renaissance a "less controversial" topic than the uncompromising, complicated art from Chicago's era.

"You can teach a Langston Hughes poem about Africa or some of the other great works of the Harlem Renaissance," he said. "But it won't raise the same kind of troubling questions that would have come out of the Black Chicago Renaissance, where you've got Arna Bontemps writing about slave revolts."

He added, "Look at the work of Charles White: what's being depicted there is a revisionist, resistant activist form of African-American history that doesn't make African Americans passive or victims. It makes them a people in struggle and essential to American history. It's a very radical idea, even today."

Dr. Margaret Burroughs, vice president of the Chicago Park District's board of commissioners and co-founder of the DuSable Museum of African American History.

A PAPER THAT STARTED A REVOLUTION:

The *Chicago Defender*'s Impact on the Black Press

By Corli Jay

Originally published in summer 2021

In Chicago, the history of the Black press taking the telling of Black stories into our own hands began with *The Conservator*, the city's first Black publication founded in 1878 by lawyer and activist Ferdinand Lee Barnett, who was also the husband of journalist and activist Ida B. Wells.

Nearly 30 years later, another Black publication would come along, not only furthering the impact of Chicago's Black press but also creating a refuge for Black Americans across the U.S.

Founded in 1905 by Robert Sengstacke Abbott, the *Chicago Defender* started as a dynamic force, used as a tool for Black progression. It spread vital information for economic opportunities and Black achievement, among other things.

In the 1920s, Black people in Chicago — and across the country — still experienced wrongful treatment such as unjust working conditions and discriminatory hiring practices. Because of this, Abbott — who initially pursued a career in law — saw a strong need for the Black community to organize for the abolition of Jim Crow laws and against the inhumane treatment of the community.

Thus, the *Chicago Defender* became his form of activism. He believed he could make more of an impact by using the press to spread news of financial opportunities, positive things happening for the everyday Black person and details on the murders of countless people at the hands of law enforcement.

Starting with a circulation of 300 papers, the *Defender's* readership rapidly grew to a circulation of 100,000 by 1917 and was the first Black newspaper to reach national distribution, according to the book *A Few Red Drops* by Claire Hartfield.

The rapid growth was fueled in part by the sharing of the paper among Black people who found the news useful and too vital to keep to themselves. The weekly paper also included job postings, train schedules, and truths about the heinous lynchings happening in the

Muhammad Ali sitting in the back of a convertible waving to a crowd during the Bud Billiken Day Parade at 39th Street and Martin Luther King Drive, Chicago, Illinois.

country. Iconic writers such as Langston Hughes and Gwedolyn Brooks were also featured in the Defender.

The *Chicago Defender* is often credited for galvanizing the Great Migration of Black people to the North, causing Chicago's Black population to nearly triple between 1910 and 1920. The publication was shared among readers by way of Black Pullman train porters and entertainers above and below the Mason-Dixon Line and was read aloud to crowds inside of barbershops, beauty salons and churches.

Since its inception, the *Defender* has become a staple in Chicago and Black history as a whole. The publication birthed the largest African-American parade in the United States, the Bud Billiken parade. "The Bud," as referred to by Chicagoans, got its start in the *Defender Junior*, the paper's children's section — formed as a youth club to inspire community involvement and uplift education. The Bud happens annually as a back-to-school celebration that has brought out all sides of the city since it first debuted in 1929.

The space the *Defender* created inspired future Black media outlets such as Johnson Publishing's *Ebony* and *Jet* magazines, the *Chicago Crusader*, and today's digital outlets like *The TRiiBE*.

In July 2019, the *Defender* stopped printing paper to become digital only. Although physical copies of the paper cease to exist, the radical spirit of the early *Chicago Defender* is prevalent in any Black outlet that does news for us, by us.

30

WHEN POLICY WAS KING:
A look into Black Chicago's numbers game

=== By Kelly Garcia ===

Originally published in summer 2021

The predecessor of the Illinois state lottery was an illegal gambling game played by Black Chicagoans called "policy." Though heavily criminalized, this quick but cheap numbers game was a boost for the local economy and Chicago's Black policy kings made sure to monopolize it.

The Father of Policy

In 1885, Samuel Young, also known as the "Father of Policy" or "Policy Sam," moved to Chicago from New Orleans. Alongside his associates, a white man named Patsy King and an Asian man named "King Foo," the trio introduced the illegal numbers game to Chicago's streets — though it wasn't initially popular.

The Jones Brothers

In its heyday, it's estimated that $25 million was being bet on Chicago's policy game. The Jones Brothers were at the top of the syndicate. Edward (Ed), George, and McKissack (Mack) Jones started a policy station at the back entrance of their Jones Brothers Tailor Shop and by 1946 were running an entire policy business enterprise in Bronzeville. Led by Ed, the brothers financed the Jones Brothers Ben Franklin Store on 47th St., then the world's only Black-owned department store. During their reign, the policy scene in Chicago was known as the center of Black business in the United States. Their time eventually came to an end after a run-in with the feds and white gangsters.

John "Mushmouth" Johnson

Known as the "Negro Gambling King of Chicago," John "Mushmouth" Johnson acquired a fortune running a policy enterprise, but not as a player — as a businessman. Born in 1857 in St. Louis, Missouri, Johnson earned the nickname "Mushmouth" for his "thick" speech. He owned a saloon called The Emporium, which became his gambling empire for 20 years, as he rose to become the king of policy. He developed strong relationships with Chicago's political machine and used his power to finance Black Chicago's entertainment hub.

Provident Hospital

Founded: **Jan. 22, 1891**
Location: **29th and Dearborn**

Provident Hospital, created as a training facility for Black nurses, was the first Black hospital in Chicago. It is widely acknowledged that Dr. Daniel Hale Williams performed the first open-heart surgery here. The hospital reopened as Provident Hospital of Cook County at 550 E. 51st Street in 1993.

Wendell Phillips Academy

Founded: **Sept 04, 1904**
Location: **244 East Pershing Road**

Chicago's first predominantly Black high school. Alums include Gwendolyn Brooks, Sam Cooke, and Dinah Washington.

The Chicago Urban League

Founded: **1916**
Location: **3032 South Wabash Avenue**

The CUL provided vital social services to a growing Black population and helped them secure employment and affordable housing.

The Chicago Bee

Founded: **1925**
Location: **3647-55 South State Street**

A Black newspaper founded by Anthony Overton to compete with the *Chicago Defender* and to appeal to middle-class Black Chicagoans.

Binga State Bank

Founded: **1908**
Location: **3422 South State Street**

Chicago's first Black banker, Jesse Binga, founded Binga State Bank, the city's first Black-owned bank in 1908. Binga opened a brick-and-mortar location on Jan. 3, 1921.

FORMATION OF BLACK INSTITUTIONS IN CHICAGO

By Tonia Hill

Originally published in summer 2021

By 1900, Black Chicago's population was in the thousands. Despite racism and discrimination Black people took what they had and made lemonade, forming one-of-a-kind cultural institutions.

View of receptionist at desk and waiting area in the Johnson Publishing Company

Class of 1904 nurses from Provident Hospital, Chicago, Illinois.

Close-up exterior view of front of the Johnson Publishing Company building at 820 South Michigan

JOHNSON PUBLISHING COMPANY

Supreme Life Insurance Company

Founded: **1919**
Location: **3501 South King Drive**

Founded initially as the Liberty Life Insurance Company by Frank L. Gillespie who wanted to offer Black people better quality life insurance.

Poro College

Founded: **1930**
Location: **4410 South King Drive**

Poro was founded in St. Louis by Annie T. Malone, and relocated to Chicago in the early 1930s. She ran her beauty empire from her mansions on King Drive. Today, Irvine C. Mollison Elementary School sits in its location.

Johnson Publishing Company

Founded: **Nov. 1942**
Location: **3501 South King Drive (original location)**

Johnson Publishing was the nation's leading Black-owned publishing firm. *Ebony* and *Jet* magazines became a fixture in the Black community. Both celebrated Black life and culture. In 1971, the company moved into its iconic 820 S. Michigan Ave. location.

Harold's Chicken Shack

Founded: **June 22, 1950**
Location: **47th and Kenwood Avenue**

Harold Pierce — a.k.a. the Fried Chicken King — started Harold's in Woodlawn. The brand is thriving. Folks all over the country get to experience mild sauce thanks to Pierce.

Soft Sheen Products Inc.

Founded: **1964**
Location: **1000 East 87th Street**

Edward and Bettiann Gardner founded Soft Sheen because there was a lack of hair products for people of color. Soft Sheen is most famous for its Jheri curl spray and activator.

OUT WEST II: A MISSISSIPPI STORY

By Tiffany Walden

Originally published in September 2018

The flight from Chicago to Memphis, Tenn., scared the hell out of us. It was a Monday afternoon in June 2018. Skies were clear. Once comfortably at cruise altitude, I fell asleep in the row ahead of *TRiiBE* co-founder Morgan Elise Johnson. An hour or so later, as the plane prepared for landing, turbulence hit bad. I woke up to the plane taking a violent dip in the middle of a menacing cloud. The full flight fell silent.

Mississippi is filled with the voices of the overlooked — the many Black folk who ended up on Chicago's West Side before and during the Great Migration, but have since been reduced to the two or three summary sentences in the sharecropping part of our school history lessons.

You know that chapter. It's after Reconstruction but right before the Civil Rights Movement. Well, that's dependent on the willingness of your teacher to improvise outside of the history book and, of course, my West Side story isn't written there. But maybe if I listen closely while in Mississippi, the omniscient roots of the trees and infinite streams of the river will hum my granny's tune.

"A whole bunch of people got right with God just now," Johnson said, laughing but serious, as we walked to the Memphis International Airport rideshare pickup zone where a huge confederate flag greeted us.

Once in the rental car, we embarked on the two-hour drive to Bolivar County, Miss. I was eager to learn more about this place on the border of the Mississippi River that, in the early 1900s, was brimming with a profitable agricultural system built on the backs of Black tenant farmers, although with little to no reward for them at the end of each harvest. My granny grew up there.

At the start of the 20th century, Bolivar County was home to 5,515 farms, totaling about 246,000 acres in land; a value of excess $5.8 million. That's about $211 million in today's money. Might I add, Bolivar County's population in 1900 saw 4,017 whites to 31,230 coloreds, a disparity unexplained and unaccounted for in Dunbar Rowland's cyclopedic description of a seemingly successful county.

My granny never talked about Mississippi, at least with me. She died in December 2006. I was 18 years old at the time. Later in 2016, in a casual conversation with her oldest child, my uncle Sunny, I heard a story about my ancestors for the first time. He reminisced about the two times my granny took him and his little

brother to the farm in Mississippi. My uncle didn't remember much about his great-grandmother, whom he affectionately called Big Mama, mostly because he grew up in a time when kids were seen and not heard. So he rarely, if ever, asked questions.

"I think the farm was right outside of Clarksdale. When we was kids, every summer we was on the Greyhound bus or train going somewhere, to where we had to just sit and be quiet," he said. "[In Mississippi], we used to get up on this big ole red horse and ride into town with my grandfather, you know. Big Mama used to sit on the porch in a rocking chair with a whip. If you crossed the fence line, she popped the whip at you. After a couple of times, they didn't take me back no more because of my mouth, you know, being down there with them white people."

Despite the bad things I had heard about Mississippi as a kid, my granny's birthplace had become a mystifying mecca that I needed to know more about. I wanted to know where I came from. I wanted to know what my granny's childhood was like, and why she never talked about her father's death.

Until my uncle Sunny's funeral in November 2017, I had never seen pictures of her before July 1960.

That's when she moved into the house I later grew up in on the 4000 block of West Lexington Street on Chicago's West Side. Why is that? Did she look like me as a young girl? Did she create imaginary worlds with her dolls like I did? The day she died is the day I realized I didn't ask the right questions when I interviewed her during my high school AP U.S. History class project. She was 85 years old at the time, and couldn't remember exactly how to spell the name of the small town she grew up in.

A right turn off Blues Highway 61 took us down the winding road to Alligator, a Bolivar County town of maybe 200 people. The buildings reminded me of those in the old westerns my uncle Billy used to watch at my granny's house. Except, there weren't any cowboys or watchful old men lounging around on the front porches of these businesses. The streets were lonely and the buildings soulless.

We came here to find the cemetery. Morgan's great-grandmother, Josephine Brown, was buried here, coincidentally, a mere 15-minute drive from my granny's birthplace in Deeson. It's why our friendship has always felt deeper than us.

We drove up to a couple of homes in Alligator to ask the Black women on porches where the cemeteries were. There's only one, they said, and it's right next to the old church on Front Street. We saw the church, parked and looked over the few grave markers in front of it. None of them were Josephine Brown.

So we got back in the car and rode round some more, hoping to find the real cemetery. That's when we ran into a Black man who directed us back to the old church. It's the only cemetery he knows of, too. How could a town founded in the 1800s, once home to 1,000 people and three bustling cotton gins, have so few graves? When the Black man caught up with us at the old church, he told us his name was Mayor Tommie Brown, the first Black mayor of Alligator.

"We might be some kin," he said. Morgan smiled. She told him that we were looking for her great-grandmother's headstone. So he dialed up some of his relatives

to see if the names Josephine Brown or her daughter, Morgan's grandmother Azella McClinton, rang a bell. He told us to look around behind the church.

"There's more back there," Mayor Brown said.

On first sight, there wasn't much back there —mostly overgrown foliage and woods appropriate for the setting of a scary movie. We crept to the edge of the forest and discovered one tombstone. Then another covered in weeds. I grabbed a stick and pushed away more dead leaves to unveil more flat headstones. None were Josephine Brown.

Morgan then noticed a few more graves deep inside the woods but we couldn't take a chance on going in there. There was minimal sunlight inside, and the real possibility of snakes and who knows what else. The old church and cemetery didn't give the answers we were looking for.

I thought every town would look like Alligator. But Deeson, about 12 miles west of Alligator, looked like a ghost town. Blades of grass stretched for as far as my eyes could see. A handful of wood-framed homes lined Deeson's one winding road. A barn with the words "Deeson, MS" and three silos with "Old Delta Farms" painted across them were the only indicators of place. We had just discovered the 1927 record book for the Deeson School, and my granny's name was in there. But looking around Deeson, there was no evidence of a school ever being here.

Unlike Alligator, there weren't any Black women sitting on porches or the occasional Black man walking down the street in Deeson. It was still, quiet, except for the birds chirping in the distance and the bees buzzing by. I stood near the "Deeson, MS" barn with my eyes closed. I tried listening for my granny's voice but I couldn't hear her.

After my granny died, I searched the internet for Decen, Miss. That's how she spelled it for me. But

May 19, 2006:
AP U.S. History
Oral History
Project

Interviewer:
Tiffany Walden

Subject: Irene
Johnson
(Buchanan)

Irene Buchanan, photographed in 1942 at Daisy Studio in Memphis, Tennessee

When and where were you born?
Decen, Mississippi on April 4, 1921

When did you move from Mississippi?
In 1940. We moved to Tennessee.

Why Tennessee? Parents went there?
My father died when I was 7 years old. My momma and everybody moved to Tennessee. You followed your family.

Can you explain your experience in sharecropping?
It was all fieldwork. We lived on the farm that we picked cotton on.

What was a typical day like?
Got up in the morning, went to school. Came home and did chores. We had to wash dishes, fix dinner, clean up... we didn't sleep all day like y'all do today. After that, we would do our homework.

What was it like working for whites?
It was alright. They didn't bother me. I worked for some when we moved to Clarkes, Mississippi. I did some babysitting and did laundry.

nothing came up online for Decen. I tried again in 2013. That time, Google threw me a lifeline: *did you mean Deeson, Mississippi?* Shit, yes!

Wikipedia defined it as an unincorporated community, smaller than cities such as Rosedale and towns like Alligator, but not yet a ghost town like Mound Landing, a former cotton plantation with one of the largest slave populations in the U.S. that was later wiped out by the Great Mississippi Flood of 1927.

By the end of the 1920s, Deeson's 8,800 acres was home to Delta Farms Company. It was one of two land extensions for the British-owned Delta and Pine Land Company in nearby Scott, the country's largest plantation with 38,000 acres worth $5 million at the time.

I searched for my granny's parents in the 1920 U.S. Census but didn't have enough information about their whereabouts and parents to find them. I knew her father wouldn't be in the 1940 U.S. Census because he died when my granny was seven years old, around the time of the Great Mississippi Flood of 1927. On April 21 of that year, the levees broke, sending flood waters across the Delta. The flood displaced 637,000 people in Arkansas, Mississippi and Louisiana. It's listed as one of the country's greatest natural disasters.

Much like recovery efforts for Hurricane Katrina in 2006, racist practices and scandal prevailed during Red Cross's recovery in 1927. Black journalists in Chicago reported on the slave-like conditions for Negroes "detained in outdoor camps on the levee" and forced to work without pay or much food.

"If casual reports that the National Guard had been ordered to "shoot to hit" and "show no mercy" did not provoke public suspicion of mistreatment, J. Winston Harrington's May 7 exposé in the Chicago Defender brought to light the "peonage" of Mississippi's "Jim Crow relief camps." In large print, the paper described "Refugees herded like cattle to stop escape from peonage," forced to wear numbered tags on their shirt to ensure their easy identification. Harrington had been informed by Mr. Del Weber, a white Greenville resident who witnessed black refugees
being detained. Harrington decried the presence of the National Guard, which earlier that week shot a black refugee from Cary, Mississippi "when he attempted to take food and clothing into a relief camp occupied by members of our Race." A white worker declared that the death would be a "lesson for the rest of the Niggers."

— Source: "The Red Cross Is Not All Right!" Herbert Hoover's Concentration Camp Cover Up In The 1927 Mississippi Flood by Myles McMurchy

———————————————

Did my granny's father die during the flood? Was he detained and forced to work in one of these Jim Crow relief camps? Was he lynched or murdered? I haven't been able to find a record of his death.

A sharp pain shot across my chest as we turned right onto the dirt path leading to the Mississippi River in Bolivar County. I *had* to get to the river. I wanted so badly to submerge myself in the stories it told. But, I was scared. Morgan could feel my fear.

"Are there spirits here?" she asked. "Definitely," I replied, peering into the shadows that lurked in the marshes and leafy canopies surrounding us.

We'd come to the end of the dirt road. And there was no telling what lay ahead. It was here that we had to make a choice: do we get out of the car and tread uncertain ground, or turn back?

As we turned around, the souls of the River loosened their grips. But the guilt of not asking vital questions will linger forever. We drove with the incessant ringing of silence, resounding from the lost parts of us.

What are the names of your parents?
Ned and Nancy Johnson.

Any siblings?
I am the oldest of three. It was me, Katherine and Oscar.

After Tennessee, where did you go?
My momma moved to Cleveland in 1943. I left Billy and Sidney with my momma and moved to

Did the riots and stuff sca[...] you?
Nah. They had riots over here on Madison. It used t[...] be real nice but they tore [...] up.

...liceman arresting man in
...e wake of the riots that
...upted following the assas-
...nation of Dr. Martin Luther
...ng, Jr., in Chicago, Illinois,
...pril 1968.

John C. Robinson

Janet Bragg

Cornelius Coffey

How two Chicago auto mechanics founded America's first Black-operated airport

By Ade D. Adeniji

Originally published in November 2022

In 2021, Elizabeth "Bessie" Coleman was honored with an exhibit at Chicago's O'Hare International Airport, marking 100 years since the late aviatrix obtained her international pilot's license—becoming the first African-American woman to do so. But while Coleman looms large in Black history and Black Chicago, two little-known Chicago auto mechanics-turned-aviators —inspired by her story — launched the country's first Black-owned airport. Along the way, they paved the way for Black aviators, including the Tuskegee Airmen.

Cornelius Coffey and John C. Robinson were working in Detroit for an automobile company when they saw a newspaper headline noting that Coleman had died in a plane crash.

"'Why can't a Black man fly a plane, too?' they asked. And so they decided to pick up where she left off," said Tyrone Haymore, a historian and curator at Robbins Historical Society & Museum, located just outside of Chicago.

Born in the Deep South in the early 1900s, Coffey, who graduated from Tuskegee Institute in 1920, and Robinson followed a familiar northward path of the Great Migration. The men headed to Detroit and then Chicago, having applied to Curtiss-Wright Aeronautical University to make their aviation dream a reality.

But when they arrived at the school, they were turned away, according to Haymore. Coffey filed a lawsuit, alleging discrimination, while Robinson took a job as a Curtiss-Wright janitor, peering into classes and rummaging through trash while piecing together class notes that had been tossed.

Haymore, a South Side native, learned about this history firsthand from Coffey during the 1980s. Coffey passed away in 1994 but for his final decade of life, Haymore said, the two would get together every other week. Haymore grew up around the same area near the 4000 block of South Indiana Avenue where Coffey and Robinson set up their auto shop to make extra cash.

At that auto shop, Coffey and Robinson eventually ordered a Heath Parasol, a build-it-yourself airplane that arrived in their garage for $300—the equivalent of about $3,000 in today's dollars, Haymore said. The other critical part of the plane—the motor—cost an additional $300, which they could not afford. So they put together the plane and rolled the dice with another kind of engine.

"Robinson looked through the airplane manual, and noticed that the specifications for the engine matched up almost identically with the engine that powers a motorcycle. And he just happened to have a motorcycle. So what do you think he did?" Haymore asked.

A bewildered Curtiss-Wright instructor caught wind of their project, and wanted to meet the two young Black men intending to take to the skies with no experience. The three ferried the plane to a grassy field in Washington Park, where the plane took off and flew perfectly. After that, Coffey and Robinson were admitted to Curtiss-Wright as night students, graduating within a year.

The next step for the aviators was to expand their operations to make good on Coleman's dream. In 1931, they formed the Challenger Air Pilots Association for Black pilots. They needed an airport, but when that idea was not well-received within Chicago city limits, they took their talents to Robbins, Illinois—an all-Black town whose mayor, Samuel Nichols, embraced them. Nichols' daughter, Nichelle Nichols, went on to become an actress on the TV series "Star Trek," portraying Lt. Uhura.

Volunteer laborers immediately began clearing trees and removing boulders, eventually building a hangar from stray lumber. Robbins Airport opened on 14046 S. Lawndale Ave. in 1931. The early Challenger Air Pilots Association included a dozen or so Black men and women, including Janet Bragg, a Spelman graduate and nurse; and Willa Brown, who was enrolled in a master's degree program at Northwestern University.

"These women were the first two people that Coffey and Robinson taught to fly," Haymore said. Bragg and her husband were able to purchase two airplanes for Robbins Airport. Brown, who was working at a Walgreens cafe at the time, was brought into the enterprise when she overheard Coffey and Robinson talking about aviation, Haymore said.

A violent windstorm destroyed Robbins Airport in 1933—but this act of destruction actually began new chapters for Coffey and Robinson. Coffey and Brown established the Coffey School of Aeronautics in 1938 on Harlem Avenue in an area of what is now known as Bridgeview. The school's cafe, a haven from dealing with discrimination at local restaurants, was operated by a certain civil-rights figure.

"Willa Brown was so busy operating the school. So she hired a young teenager to operate the cafe. That woman was Mamie Till," Haymore said.

As for Robinson, the more adventurous of the two, he ultimately ended up far beyond Chicago in Ethiopia,

where he helped train Haile Selassie's pilots in their ongoing conflict with Italy. Robinson died in that African country in 1954, earning the nickname "Brown Condor" for his service.

Umberto Ricco, a longtime aircraft mechanic, is also adamant about preserving and honoring this history. More than 1,500 students graduated from the Coffey School and many of them went on to fly for the legendary Tuskegee Airmen.

WHY CAN'T A BLACK MAN FLY A PLANE, TOO?"

"The HBCUs—Howard, Hampton and Tuskegee—were teaching basic flying then. But the program here in Chicago went into the advanced courses—everything you needed to know to become a military cadet," Ricco explained, adding that while he was always aware of the Tuskegee Airmen, it wasn't until he went to the Smithsonian and pored over Coffey's interviews that he began to understand the full scope of Black aviation history.

Today, Ricco runs Coffey School of Aeronautics NEXT, an after-school program for students in Chicago Public Schools that aims to continue to honor Coffey's legacy. Coffey himself taught in many vocational high schools throughout Chicago.

"There are some incredible pilots that owe their career to Mr. Coffey," added Haymore. "Did I even mention that he was the inventor of the carburetor heater for airplanes that prevented icing? He could have been a multimillionaire. But he wasn't about that."

According to the 2021 data from the U.S. Bureau of Labor Statistics, 3.9 percent of pilots and aircraft engineers in the U.S. aviation industry are Black. However, the legacies of Chicago pioneers Coffey and Robinson remind many that Black Americans also have a place in aviation.

How Black Chicago helped birth the Black Fives, the Negro league of hoops

By Ade D. Adeniji

Originally published in September 2021

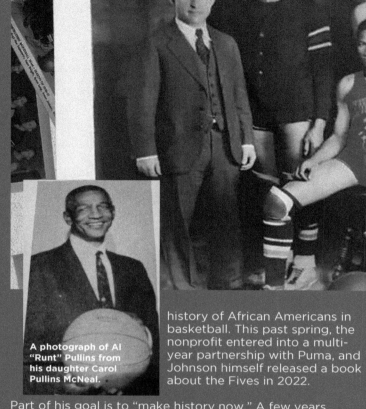

A photograph of Al "Runt" Pullins from his daughter Carol Pullins McNeal.

Isiah Thomas. Dwyane Wade. Derrick Rose. Some of the NBA's greatest players of all time call Chicago home. What is it about the Windy City that pairs so well with hardwood courts and Spalding?

Well, once upon a time during the era of segregation, early Black basketball thrived in what is known as the Black Fives era; a period of amateur, semi-professional and professional basketball between 1904 and 1946 before the launch and integration of the NBA.

Black Fives teams included the New York Renaissance, the Monticello Athletic Association of Pittsburgh, and even mighty Howard University — winners of the 1910-1911 championship, as determined by leading Black sports writers of the day. These journalists helped cohere an emerging game which, unlike the NBA today, cannot be pinned down to a unified association, location or venue.

In Chicago, a few Black Fives teams and names stand out, including the Savoy Big Five and Harlem Clowns.

"Prior to 1913, there really were no Black-controlled venues until the Wabash Avenue YMCA was built because of a matching grant from Julius Rosenwald," explains Claude Johnson, a Stanford University-trained engineer and long-time marketing executive.

Rosenwald, a prominent Jewish philanthropist and cofounder of Sears and Roebuck, deeply believed in social services and education. Inspired by Booker T. Washington, he helped launch dozens of YMCAs in Black neighborhoods. The five-story Wabash Avenue YMCA is where Carter G. Woodson proposed the idea of "Negro History Week," a precursor to Black History Month.

"And when they opened this [Wabash Avenue YMCA] up, it had a really nice gymnasium in there that was used for basketball and suddenly Black basketball in Chicago got on the map," Johnson adds.

Johnson now dedicates the bulk of his time to running the Black Fives Foundation to honor the pre-NBA history of African Americans in basketball. This past spring, the nonprofit entered into a multi-year partnership with Puma, and Johnson himself released a book about the Fives in 2022.

Part of his goal is to "make history now." A few years ago, then-Chicago Bulls star Taj Gibson and visual artist Swopes joined rising local ballplayers to create a short video that reflects on the landmark Wabash Avenue YMCA and the Black Fives history in Chicago.

One prominent Chicago basketball team from the Black Fives era is the Savoy Big Five. They took down all-Black teams including Pennsylvania's Lincoln University, Wilberforce University and the Loendi Big Five of Pittsburgh. But the Savoy Big Five are also a good example of the fusion between athletic play and other forms of entertainment, such as dance and Jazz which were part of these bonafide cultural events.

In 1927, Associated Ballrooms, Inc., a builder of a series of behemoth ballrooms in Harlem and elsewhere, signed a 30-year, $1 million lease of an entire South Side Chicago city block to build the Savoy Ballroom, according to Johnson. The likes of Louis Armstrong, Count Basie, Duke Ellington, and Ella Fitzgerald were featured acts.

The cultural venue later became the ball team's home court in 1928.

The mighty Savoy, home of sports and entertainment, stood until the early 1970s, and was located on South Parkway Boulevard (now Martin Luther King Drive) at 47th Street. The venue was large enough to accommodate 7,500 dancers. And the Savoy Big Five's first manager was Black nightclub promoter Dick "Baby Face" Hudson. He previously coached and managed an all-Black Chicago-based team named the Giles Post American Legion Five, and ended up renaming that team to the Savoy Big Five, after its ballroom sponsor.

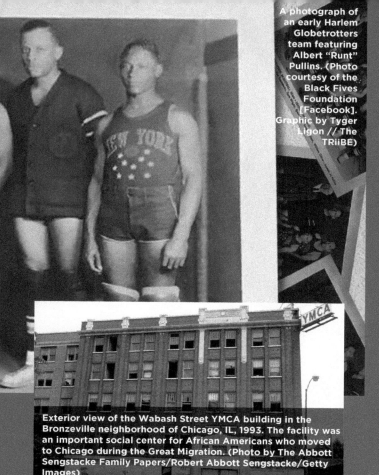

A photograph of an early Harlem Globetrotters team featuring Albert "Runt" Pullins. (Photo courtesy of the Black Fives Foundation [Facebook]. Graphic by Tyger Ligon // The TRiiBE)

Exterior view of the Wabash Street YMCA building in the Bronzeville neighborhood of Chicago, IL, 1993. The facility was an important social center for African Americans who moved to Chicago during the Great Migration. (Photo by The Abbott Sengstacke Family Papers/Robert Abbott Sengstacke/Getty Images)

the second-oldest traveling team in the country after the Globetrotters.

The Harlem Clowns took their talents far beyond Chicago, barnstorming across the country and eventually as far and wide as Canada and Japan. In those early days, Pullins' mother and aunt loaned him their car and money so that he could be on the move with the Clowns. McNeal-Smith describes it as an "Akeelah and the Bee" family affair.

On the road navigating with and without the *Green Book*, the Chicago-based Harlem Clowns arrived in sleepy towns in the Midwest, Jim Crow South, and elsewhere where they also faced and thrived against all-white competition. But the all-Black squad couldn't just go in and wallop these teams — unwise both for business and because it might trigger something such as a race riot.

"What would happen is that you would go into a small town and play predominantly-white teams, but you could not run up the score. Yes you were there for entertainment. But you also needed to leave with your safety intact," McNeal-Smith explains.

Now, some might see the Harlem Clowns and Harlem Globetrotters-type play as flirting with buffoonery at times, but McNeal-Smith aims to reframe the narrative, speaking to the truly delicate tightrope that these Black athletes had to walk.

Ultimately, McNeal-Smith calls the Clowns' play a true survival tactic that combined adept footwork, athleticism and skill — another example of the complicated strategies Black people have used to survive and thrive throughout American history.

" YOU WOULD GO INTO A SMALL TOWN AND PLAY PREDOMINANTLY-WHITE TEAMS, BUT YOU COULD NOT RUN UP THE SCORE. YES YOU WERE THERE FOR ENTERTAINMENT. BUT YOU ALSO NEEDED TO LEAVE WITH YOUR SAFETY INTACT,

Later, a faction of the Savoy Big Five became the Harlem Globetrotters when North Side Jewish businessman Abe Saperstein joined the team in the late 1920s. Some of these Trotters were born out of a squad of talented athletes from Bronzeville's Wendell Phillips High School, with one of these stars being Al "Runt" Pullins, a 5 foot 8 speedster and dead-eye shooter who refined his skills at the Wabash Y.

His daughter Carol Pullins McNeal, and granddaughter Andria McNeal-Smith, continue to keep Pullins' legacy alive and, along with Johnson, have advocated for his induction into the Naismith Memorial Basketball Hall of Fame.

At publishing time, only 12 players from the Black Fives had been posthumously inducted. Pullins was not yet one of them. In 2022, he was inducted.

Born in Louisiana, Pullins followed the common northward trajectory of the Great Migration to Chicago when he was six years old. Though away from the Jim Crow South, spaces west of State Street on Chicago's South Side were verboten.

"There were boundaries of course, but for them I think it was a full experience and they were able to test their skills. As young men, all they wanted to do is play," McNeal says, adding that the Pullins family was able to become homeowners and step into the middle class.

As captain of Wendell Phillips High School's basketball team, Pullins set a Chicago high school single-season scoring record that stood until the late 1940s and led his school as the first Black team to win a citywide championship in 1928. Later, consistent with other Black Fives figures, Pullins stepped into the role of entrepreneur and founded the Chicago-based Harlem Clowns in 1934,

"These are the things we're looking to challenge as we set the record straight," she adds.

Pullins traveled the world thanks to his hooping ability on the court and business acumen off of it. His career with the Clowns lasted until the 1970s.

"Who knew that the real OGs had already won rings in a league of their own," asks Chicago-bred rapper Lil Bibby, as he narrated the words of poet Joekenneth Museau in that Wabash Y short video released a few years ago.

Ultimately, the Black Fives is another example of Black excellence on the court, and leadership and activism off of it. So when detractors tell current NBA players to stick to hoops, the legacy of the Black Fives in Chicago and beyond reminds us that this can never be the case.

The Committee for a Black Mayor has been established to choose a mayoral candidate for the next election, and the group holds a press conference at 4859 South Wabash Avenue, Chicago, Illinois.

TAPPING INTO
POWER

1961 – 1990

An African American man holds up a sign that reads Black Power at the Cicero March in Cicero, Illinois, 1966.

Fred Hampton, social activist and chairman of Illinois chapter of the Black Panther Party, speaking at event, Chicago, Illinois.

Reverend Jesse Jackson speaks to students, teachers, and parents after a recent boycott was suspended

BLACK LABOR MOVEMENTS

By Tonia Hill

Originally published in summer 2021

In late 1965, Rev. Dr. Martin Luther King Jr. arrived in Chicago to join the Chicago Freedom Movement, launched by community activists to confront the city's deep-seated racism and discrimination in housing, education and employment. The Movement was instrumental in Congress' passing of the Fair Housing Act of 1968.

Local activists and organizers involved in the Chicago Freedom Movement, including Civil Rights leader Rev. Jesse Jackson, educator and organizer Albert "Al" Raby, and labor and Civil Rights leader Rev. Dr. Addie L. Wyatt later joined forces with grassroots organizations to elect Harold Washington as Chicago's first Black mayor in 1983.

Rev. Jesse Jackson

A prominent Civil Rights leader, closely associated with Martin Luther King Jr. and the Southern Christian Leadership Conference (SCLC), who led the Chicago chapter of Operation Breadbasket from 1966. He founded Operation PUSH and the National Rainbow Coalition, which merged into Rainbow/PUSH (People United to Save/Serve Humanity) in 1996. Operation Breadbasket fought racist hiring, promoted Black businesses, and advocated for job opportunities in Chicago. PUSH organized a massive voter registration campaign involving 30+ local organizations and Black businesses, registering 100,000 new minority voters, setting the stage for a potential Black mayoral candidate in Chicago.

Al Raby

An educator and Civil Rights activist, Raby convened Chicago's Civil Rights coalition (Coordinating Council of Community Organizations), helped to organize the massive 1963 boycott of Chicago Public Schools, and was instrumental in persuading Dr. Martin Luther King Jr. and the SCLC to help in the ongoing effort to improve housing conditions for Black people in Chicago during the Chicago Freedom Movement. He also served as Harold Washington's historic mayoral campaign manager.

Renault Robinson

A former Chicago police officer who founded the Afro-American Patrolmen's League, Renault got Soft Sheen Products founder Ed Gardner to craft advertisements for the "Come Alive October 5" campaign, a citywide voter registration initiative, and solicited Black businesses to fund Washington's campaign. He served as chairman of the Chicago Housing Authority under

Lutrelle "Lu" Palmer

A journalist, syndicated columnist, newspaper publisher and radio commentator, he became an outspoken supporter of Washington and would mention him on his radio show; he later became Washington's speechwriter and campaign manager.

Gus Savage

Democratic Congressman for Illinois' 2nd District and publisher of the Citizen Newspapers, a chain of community weeklies, he also led campaigns in Chicago for Black liberation, fair housing, and Civil Rights. He managed Washington's first bid for mayor in 1977, and helped Washington win the 1983 election.

Doctor Martin Luther King, Jr., Al Raby (second from right), and fellow activists walk up Independence Boulevard to apartments at 3808 West Fillmore Street, Chicago, Illinois. King and Raby inspect holes in apartment walls and show rent strike signs.

Rev. Dr. Addie L. Wyatt

A union, religious and Civil Rights leader, Wyatt was the first female president of a local chapter of the United Packinghouse Workers of America, was involved in the Chicago Freedom Movement and also a member of the Washington for Women committee. She was also part of a group that sought to elect a Black mayoral candidate in 1977.

The Committee for a Black Mayor has been established to choose a mayoral candidate for the next election, and the group holds a press conference at 4859 South Wabash Avenue, Chicago, Illinois. Members of the committee include: Charles A. Hayes, Thomas Todd, Tommy Brisco, Reverend Clay Evans, and Nancy Jefferson

Nancy Jefferson

A community activist known as the "Joan of Arc of the West Side" who worked tirelessly to improve the condition of people living out West, she was head of the Midwest Community Council, which led the charge to rebuild Garfield Park after the 1968 riots. She served as co-chair of the Women for Washington committee, which organized a major campaign rally for Washington in January 1983 at Liberty Baptist Church.

IV. TAPPING INTO POWER

1961–1990

by Matt Harvey

Chicago playwright Lorraine Hansberry's 1959 play, *A Raisin in the Sun,* tells the story of the Youngers, a Black family in Chicago trying to move from their apartment in the South Side slums to a new home in an all-white neighborhood.

The fictional Younger family represented a true-to-life depiction of what reality was becoming for Black families in mid-20th century Chicago— their housing options were typically limited to a run-down apartment in the overcrowded city slums, or an uncomfortable life under the constant threat of physical harm from racist neighbors in white neighborhoods.

Throughout the 1960s and 1970s, redlining continued to funnel an increasing population of Black people into severely overcrowded areas in the city, including Chicago Housing Authority (CHA) housing projects such as the Robert Taylor Homes and the Cabrini–Green Homes, where crime and unemployment rates were increased. The move toward de-industrialization made formal education a greater necessity, yet Black kids in Chicago couldn't get a fair shake at school.

But this timeline of Black Chicago between 1960 and 1990 isn't the story of the fall of Black Metropolis. The story of this timeline is tapping into power to fight against institutionalized racism.

1961

Hundreds of Native Americans came to Chicago in 1961 for the American Indian Chicago Conference held at the University of Chicago. This sparked the mobilization of American Indian activists and the Red Power Movement.

Two people heading to a pow wow at University of Chicago's Stagg Field at East 55th Street, Chicago, Illinois.

1963

In 1963, the Coordinating Council of Community Organizations (CCCO) organized a school boycott to protest the inequities between the conditions of white schools versus Black ones. In Black schools, the overcrowding was so bad that instead of pouring money into a permanent solution, Chicago Public Schools (CPS) Superintendent Benjamin Willis deployed temporary aluminum mobile structures, dubbed "Willis Wagons," by organizers. In 1964, CCCO elected a schoolteacher named Al Raby to lead the organization as its convener.

1965

Jeffery Pub opened in 1965. It is one of the oldest LGBTQ+ clubs in the country. Today, located at 7041 S. Jeffery, it is Chicago's only Black-owned gay club.

1968

Chairman Fred Hampton & the Black Panthers

View of Bobby Rush, Deputy Minister of Defense, and Fred Hampton, Deputy Chairman, of the Illinois Black Panther Party posing at the Party's headquarters, 2350 West Madison Street, Chicago, Illinois, 1969.

In 1966, Maywood teenager and aspiring law student Fred Hampton became intrigued by readings on socialism and the work of communist leaders including Che Guevara and Ho Chi Minh. While a youth leader of the NAACP's west suburban branch, he began to take notice of the Black Panther Party movement being led by Huey P. Newton and Bobby Seale in Oakland, Calif.

The Panthers' politics — which were much more radical and socialist than the NAACP — resonated with Hampton. In 1968, he and Bobby Rush founded the Illinois Chapter of the Black Panther Party (ILBPP).

Hampton served as deputy chairman, and Rush became the deputy minister of defense, and within four months of establishing the chapter, they had a membership of more than 300.

The ILBPP set up and oversaw free "survival programs," including food, clothing, home repairs, a Peoples' Medical Care Center and the Free Breakfast for School Children Program. Hampton's socialist politics inspired him to approach the liberation fight from a lens that understood American capitalism and imperialism as the Panthers' primary adversary.

This class-based approach, along with Hampton's innate leadership ability and charisma, allowed the ILBPP to build relationships with other community organizations to form the Rainbow Coalition, which included the Puerto Rican organization called the Young Lords and a white-run organization called the Young Patriots.

Hampton's rapid ascension to leadership and his favorability made him a particular threat to the U.S. government, and the FBI sought to dismantle revolutionary organizations such as the Black Panthers through their Counter Intelligence Program or COINTELPRO. On Dec. 4, 1969, 21-year-old Hampton and fellow Panther 22-year-old Mark Clark were murdered in their sleep during an FBI and Chicago Police Department (CPD) raid on Hampton's West Side apartment.

1969

In 1969, Henry Weimhoff, inspired by the Stonewall Riot, helped organize the University of Chicago Gay Liberation Front, which was absorbed into Chicago Gay Liberation the following year. The group was a more radical gay liberation organization, keeping in line with the trend of radical politics that began to take a mainstream hold (see: Black Panther Party). Later, the Third World Gay Revolution was an organization created as a caucus of Chicago Gay Liberation focused on issues faced by Black queer folk.

1970

In 1970, a former WVON-AM news reporter and substitute DJ named Don Cornelius, bothered by the lack of venues for soul music on television, came up with the idea of "Soul Train"— a music show that brought a Black nightclub to a daytime television set. With Cornelius as the maestro, "Soul Train" quickly became a local phenomenon and by 1971, it gained national syndication.

In 1970, a fight for better housing for Chicago's growing Native American population began with the Chicago Indian Village (CIV). A Menominee woman had been evicted from her Wrigleyville apartment, sparking a two-month encampment by activists at a Wrigley Field parking lot, according to the Dunn Museum. Between 1970 and 1972, CIV organizer Mike Chosa planned several different encampments across Chicagoland, all with the goal of forcing the government to address poor housing and social services for Native American people in the city.

Janet Jackson is interviewed by Don Cornelius on Soul Train episode 408, aired 12/18/1982. (Photo by Soul Train via Getty Images).

1973

Although originally named the Ebony Museum of Negro History and Art, the DuSable Museum of African American History took on the name of Chicago's first non-Indigenous settler after moving to its current Washington Park location in 1973. Founded by Margaret Burroughs, the DuSable Museum is the oldest caretaker of African-American history in the U.S.

1975

Walter Payton, a.k.a. "Sweetness," was drafted by the Chicago Bears with the fourth overall pick in the 1975 NFL draft, opening the door to a new chapter for Chicago sports. Payton is widely regarded as one of the greatest NFL players of all time, and his drafting was the first major shift in the tide for Chicago sports teams, which hadn't made much noise since the early 20th century. He helped lead the 1985 Bears to their Super Bowl XX championship, retired with multiple franchise and league records in 1987 and was inducted into the NFL Hall of Fame.

Many laws were passed in response to the Red Power movement, one of the most notable being the Indian Self-Determination and Education Assistance Act of 1975, which rejected paternalistic policies and gave Native Americans control of their own education.

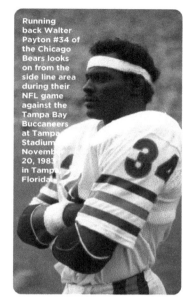

Running back Walter Payton #34 of the Chicago Bears looks on from the side line area during their NFL game against the Tampa Bay Buccaneers at Tampa Stadium November 20, 1983 in Tampa, Florida.

1990

By 1990, Black people represented the largest racial group in the city, accounting for about 39% of Chicago residents.

1983

After a grassroots campaign mobilized more than 100,000 new registered voters, Harold Washington became Chicago's first Black mayor in 1983. Washington was a mayor of the people, among many of his accomplishments — won in spite of hardline opposition from a bloc of white aldermen in the City Council — were opening the city budget process for public input, fighting to redistrict wards providing more Black and Latinx representation, and creating the Ethics Commission to check the power of the city's administration. Washington died of a sudden heart attack on Nov. 5, 1987, six months into his second term.

Harold Washington standing at a podium in front of numerous microphones, circa 1987.

1984

With the third pick in the 1984 NBA Draft, the Chicago Bulls selected Michael Jordan of the University of North Carolina-Chapel Hill. From the late 1980s through the 1990s, the most famous person in the world was a Black dude synonymous with Chicago. Jordan was so cold, they put a statue of him outside of the United Center after only half of his six NBA Championship wins.

1986

After coming to Chicago from Baltimore in 1984, TV reporter-turned talk-show host Oprah Winfrey started the "The Oprah Winfrey Show" in 1986, which quickly became one of the most popular talk shows on TV. That same year, she founded Harpo Productions Inc. She built the production studio on the Near West Side, and employed nearly 200 Chicagoans.

1989

In the 1980s, Robert Ford, Trent Adkins and Lawrence Warren felt there was a void in the publishing world. They filled that void in 1989 by creating *Thing*, a magazine centering the specific experiences and contributions of gay Black men. With a small, mostly volunteer staff, they published articles, photographs and artwork that captured LGBTQ+ life. Through 1993, they distributed thousands of copies worldwide.

The Seeley Club

Peak popularity: 1960s **Location**: 2026 W. Madison St.

A 25-foot wide storefront lounge under two floors of apartments, —The Seeley Club was a West Side neighborhood staple. Anyone could be found partying any given night over a beer and a sandwich cooked on the large industrial grill. On December 11,1965 the club shuttered after a fatal fire.

Ray's Cotanga Lounge

Peak popularity: 1960s **Location:** Cermak and Kostner

The sultry R&B soul lounge is remembered fondly by longtime West Siders as a place where a girl could sit and have an older man buy her a cold Champale. "Back then the neighborhood was self-sufficient," said Linda Brunson, a North Lawndale resident since the 1960s who also frequented the lounge. Each night of the week catered to blue collar workers from different companies such as CTA and Western Electric with discounts. Neighborhood teens would watch local acts perform and then walk a few feet back to their homes.

The High Chaparral

Peak popularity: 1970s **Location:** 7740 S. Stony Island Ave.

Proclaimed the "Midwest's Largest Nite Club" by owners, the High Chaparral boasted prolific guests such as The Jackson Five, B.B. King, Ray Charles and The Ohio Players. Guests clad in silk scarves and bell-bottoms donning silk fans enjoyed cocktails and Schlitz beers while seated on wicker furniture.

Taste Entertainment Center

Peak popularity: 1980s **Location:** 63rd and Lowe, Englewood

When the large metal garage doors went up, so did the lights at Taste Entertainment Center. Guests from all over the city would fill the 13,500-square-foot behemoth of a club. Seated at the same tables as Chicagoans were stars such as Muhammad Ali. Wedding receptions, worldwide steppers contests and fights as legendary as Evander Holyfield v. George Foreman were just a few of the occasions celebrated at the famed Englewood club.

The Warehouse

Peak popularity: 1970s, 80s **Location:** 206 S. Jefferson St.

A massive three-story factory building with an intense crowd of mostly gay Black and Latino men, The Warehouse was the first place DJ Freddie Knuckles experimented with disco, soul and European electronic music spawning the genre of house music. In this sweaty, dark, industrial haunt, queer folks of color danced away the pressures of the outside world.

GET UP OFFA THAT THANG:
A glimpse into Black Chicago party culture
By Natalie Frazier

Originally published in summer 2021

This map is both a guide and a lively requiem to Black lounge culture in Chicago from the 1960s to the 2000s. Despite ongoing volatile political economic and social conditions, Black people have been enjoying themselves, fashioning world-class spaces out of dumps and creating an unprecedented lounge and club culture since they arrived in Chicago.

Teams compete in a soul train dance contest at High Chapparal.

Chic Ricks

Peak popularity: 1980s **Location:** South Loop

A storefront club in the underdeveloped South Loop, Chic Ricks was "thee joint" for young urban professionals in the city. Over an island bar, bartenders served partygoers old fashioneds and rum and cokes. With a small admission fee and a desire to dance, guests would enter the small disco room in the back and jam to funky hits from Funkadelic, Earth Wind & Fire and Midnight Star.

The Nimbus

Peak popularity: 1980s **Location:** Dolton

Tucked in an old hotel in a small suburb right outside of Chicago, The Nimbus was named top 3 discos in the world by *Playboy* in 1979. The dance floor boasted large spinning glass pyramids that were lit by a flashing, multi-color dance floor. People from all over the city paid $5 to have the night of their lives at The Nimbus.

Touch Of The Past

Peak popularity: 1990s, 2000s **Location:** Bellwood

A stone's throw from Chicago's West Side, this Bellwood staple hosts birthday bashes, open mics, Super Bowl parties and live bands. Over Remy Martin and Moet drink specials, styrofoam container jerk chicken dinners and stepping playlists, Chicago's rich club culture thrives.

50 Yard Line

Peak popularity: late 1970s, 80s **Location:** 69 E. 75th St.

"The Fifty" is home to Chicago's steppers. The lounge has a conventional sports bar and grill complete with a long bar and TVs, however, it attracts sophisticated and serious dancers. After Saturday's Stepper Brunches, guests can head down the street to the iconic Lem's BBQ.

E2

Peak popularity: 2000s **Location:** 2347 S. Michigan Ave.

This concert hall-esque second floor club sat above Epitome, an upscale steak and seafood restaurant. The club advertised its dance parties, which were often described as rowdy, over radio stations. In 2003, the iconic life of the club was cut short after a fatal stampede.

MEET US AT THE PARK:
BLACK CHICAGOANS STAY TURNING CITY PARKS INTO OUR OWN BACKYARD PARTY

By Natalie Frazier

Originally published in summer 2021

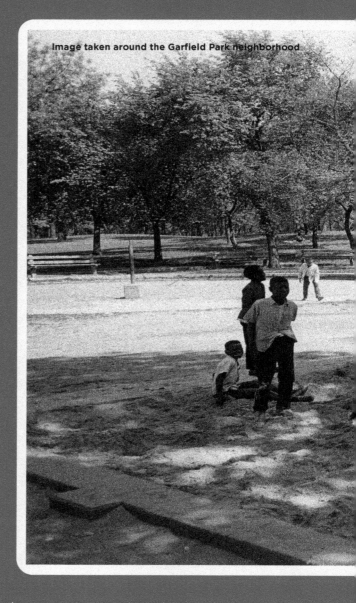

Image taken around the Garfield Park neighborhood

Chicago's beautiful urban parks were introduced in 1891 when J. Frank Foster, then-superintendent of Chicago's South Park System, argued the working class deserved spaces for passive recreation and picnicking. Black folks who had recently migrated from the South immediately recognized the value in these green spaces. Before 1931, the city opened only one playground in Chicago's Black Belt, where migrants were concentrated, so Black Chicagoans were forced to risk their lives and safety to use the city's first public spaces.

White Chicagoans reacted to Black people's use of the city's parks and beaches with racist tension and violence. In the five years before the Chicago Race Riots of 1919, white people attacked Black recreators at nearly a dozen parks, playgrounds and beaches on the South Side. The 1919 Riots began in July when a white mob killed a 17-year-old Black boy at the 29th St. Beach.

By the 1960s, Chicago's Black population had grown exponentially and white people had altogether deserted urban areas surrounding parks such as Washington Park, Grant Park, Garfield Park and Jackson Park. As the population grew, Black folks became more comfortable in the urban parks right outside of their homes.

For decades, Black people have been fellowshipping at "The Circle" in Garfield Park on the West Side. In the 60s, park-goers may have been young women walking through the park on their way to church. In the 70s and 80s, they may've been teens affiliated with the Vice Lords or Four Corner Hustlers. By the 90s, men sitting in their parked, shiny rides on Lake Street might've seen Chicago rapper Twista driving past. Today, Garfield Park hosts back to school drives, music video shoots and barbeques for lost loved ones daily. Guests check-in at "Garfield Park" on social media platforms such as Facebook to make known they're, "Chilling at The Circle."

Jackson Park sits by the lake in Woodlawn. Since the 1990s, entertainment group Chosen Few DJs has thrown an annual house music picnic in Jackson Park. Even though the even draws thousands of Black Americans to the park, it always feels more like an intimate picnic. Groups of friends, gathe under their own gazebos and seated in beach chairs arou smoking grills, each has their own personal party amid the larger celebration. Jackson Park's beach location also mak it a prime grilling and fishing spot all summer long. Black Chicagoans have also been fishing in the Jackson Park ha and other South Side beaches for smelt, steelheads, crapp and salmon for generations.

Every August, the Bud Billiken Parade winds its way throu Washington Park, which hosts celebrations of Black cultu and arts all summer long. The International Festival of Life has filled Washington Park with Black Caribbean music an culture every July Fourth weekend since the 1990s, and the African Festival of Arts, held in the park on Labor Day weekend since 1989, was the city's first festival of African culture when it started. The DuSable Museum of African American History has been located in Washington Park si 1973.

In all of the urban parks in between and beyond Garfield a Jackson Park, Black life and leisure is happening everyday

Chosen Few DJ Jesse Saunders performing at the 2019 picnic and festival. Photo by Morgan Elise Johnson/*The TRiiBE.*

The crowd enjoying a performance at the Chosen Few DJ festival. Photo by Morgan Elise Johnson/*The TRiiBE*

Members of the Blackstone Rangers gang posed in front of a boarded-up wall tagged with the word Blackstone, Chicago, Illinois, July 1, 1968.

THE REVOLUTIONARY COLUMN
THE WAR ON GANGS STUNTED OUR GROWTH

By Bella BAHHS   *Originally published in summer 2021*

"The Revolutionary Column," a series by raptivist Bella BAHHS where she spits revolutionary commentary on politics and pop culture.

In the 1960s, Black youth-led street gangs on Chicago's West and South sides were institutions. They opened businesses and recreational centers, were awarded job contracts and won scholarships to Dartmouth College.

They also worked with Dr. Martin Luther King Jr. and the Southern Christian Leadership Conference (SCLC) to spearhead the Chicago Freedom Movement, while protesting housing injustices and demanding more union jobs for African Americans.

Black street gangs were well on their way to becoming political powerhouses in a racially segregated city run by European immigrants who were hell-bent on defending their turf.

Like the Italian, German, Jewish, Polish and Irish youth-led street gangs that came before them, these tough and territorial tribes of young Black men—namely North Lawndale's Conservative Vice Lords (CVL) and Woodlawn's Black P. Stone Nation (BPSN)—were on track to transform themselves and their communities through Chicago politics.

But the revolutionary potential they harnessed to challenge and circumvent the city's power structure posed too big a threat to Chicago's most notorious gang leader of them all — then-Mayor Richard J. Daley. An Irish gangster, Daley used city power to serve and protect the interests of his community of racist, violent and politically savvy Catholic immigrants.

Long before Daley was first elected mayor in 1955, he was president of an Irish-Catholic street gang, the Hamburg Athletic Club — infamous for instigating the deadliest anti-Black race riot in Chicago's history on the South Side during the summer of 1919, when he was 17.

In the early years of the 20th century, many "athletic clubs" such as the Hamburgs were sponsored by Chicago's machine politicians and were instrumental in getting out the vote by any means necessary, including through bribes, intimidation and physical violence.

Another mostly Irish gang, the Ragen Colts, was sponsored by Cook County Commissioner Frank Ragen and became notorious bootleggers after joining forces with Al Capone and the Chicago mob known as the Outfit.

The Colts and Hamburgs are said to have invented the drive-by shooting in 1919 when they drove their cars into Bronzeville shooting at Black residents.

Many politically connected white athletic club gang members went on to become police officers, aldermen, prosecutors, judges, politicians and other government employees. In this way, gang culture is deeply embedded into Chicago politics. Unfortunately for the newly emerging Black gangs of the 1950s and 1960s, white gangs had already claimed their territory in city governance and were determined to keep Blacks out.

Young Black revolutionary gang leaders, such as the Stones' Jeff Fort, who were inspired by the budding Black Power Movement, earned themselves some powerful enemies when they decided to organize for true control over their communities and representation in City Hall.

In 1967, both the Stones and Vice Lords campaigned against Daley in his fourth bid for reelection. And not coincidentally, that same year, the Chicago Police Department established its first Gang Intelligence Unit (GIU) to monitor and infiltrate Black youth street organizations.

Leaders of the Stones and Devil's Disciples — which later became the Gangster Disciples — were hired by The Woodlawn Organization (TWO) in 1967 to run a nearly $1 million government grant program designed to engage and train 800 out-of-school youth. Daley was furious that the funds from the federal Office of Economic Opportunity bypassed City Hall and went directly to TWO.

He did everything in his power to sabotage the program and refused to approve a program director for more than two months. And when the program finally started, Daley's GIU detectives routinely surveilled and raided the Stones' training centers that TWO had opened in Woodlawn.

50

Senate committee hearings on the TWO program began on June 28, 1968, in Washington D.C. Fort and other leaders of the Stones were eventually charged by the federal government with mismanagement of funds, extortion and conspiring to defraud the U.S. government.

Members of the GIU testified against the gang members, claiming that no training was happening in the program and the Stones were using the government grant to line their pockets and fund their criminal activities. Fort was convicted and sentenced to five years in federal prison.

And just like that, Daley didn't have to worry about gangs receiving government funding in his city without his approval anymore. The Stones' reputation was so tarnished by the trial that funding for their community outreach and development programs ceased almost immediately.

Furthermore, after the trial, it was considered bad business to invest in Black street gangs or try to aid the misguided youth in actualizing their potential to evolve and become architects of community construction. Newly forming relationships between philanthropists, corporate giants, reformers and Black youth gangs were irreparably harmed.

Across town on the West Side, the Vice Lords had been raking in grants from the likes of the Rockefeller Foundation, the Ford Foundation, the U.S. Department of Labor, the Jessie Ball DuPont Fund and the Sears-Roebuck Foundation.

With this funding, from 1967 to 1969, Vice Lords, Inc. opened at least five businesses in North Lawndale, including: The African Lion, an Afro-centric clothing store; Teen Town, a youth-centered ice cream parlor; The House of Lords, a recreation center for teens; Art and Soul, an art center for youth opened in collaboration with the Museum of Contemporary Art, the University of Illinois and the Illinois Sesquicentennial Commission; and two Tastee Freez franchises.

After the trial, although the Vice Lords had nothing to do with the TWO program scandal, their funding was cut off too. All Black gangs were bad business and never to be socially accepted through political organizing like their Irish, Jewish and Italian predecessors.

And in 1969, Daley and Cook County State's Attorney Edward Hanrahan declared a full out "War on Gangs," specifically targeting Black and brown youth organizations that threatened the Irish mob's stronghold on the Democratic machine—including the

Stones, Vice Lords, Devil's Disciples and the Black Panther Party. The Panthers were actually a political organization and not a street gang, but that just made them even bigger targets for Daley and his henchmen.

It was in the context of Daley's War on Gangs that Edward Hanrahan, CPD, the GIU and the FBI conspired to murder 21-year-old Fred Hampton and 22-year-old Mark Clark of the Illinois Black Panther Party.

The War on Gangs deemed all young Black street organizers — and Black youth in general—absolute and irredeemable criminals undeserving of empathy, freedom, juvenile leniency or their lives. And from then on, gangs were hailed as the most serious crime problem in the city.

Today, when violence in Black and brown Chicago neighborhoods is categorized as "gang related," it absolves the city officials from taking responsibility for constructing racial ghettos and designated pockets of poverty.

Meanwhile, Daley and top city officials were running the biggest hiring fraud operation in Chicago history, awarding jobs, promotions and favors to their politically connected friends and associates—to their gang members.

The Vice Lords occupy Our Lady of Providence Academy at 410 South Albany Avenue, Chicago, Illinois.

WHEN THE WHOLE WORLD WAS WATCHING, THE CHICAGO POLICE RIOTED

By Monroe Anderson

Originally published in June 2020

Just like what we experienced in June 2020, 1968 was a generational sea change in America. It was when the Civil Rights Movement was muscled out by Black Power. When there was a wave of sea-to-shining-sea riots. It was a time when fearful mothers watched as their draft-age sons — whose fathers were not Fred Trump, wealthy enough to buy them a 4-F deferment — were shipped off to a foreign land, where they would risk life or limb to fight in Vietnam's civil war. There were monumental anti-war protest marches on Washington, D.C., and cities across the nation. Chicago was one of those cities.

In 2020, settled in place, I was captive to all five of my TV sets as I moved from one room to the next watching breaking news reports. Watching cell-phone recordings from May 2020 of George Floyd begging former Minneapolis Police Department Officer Derek Chauvin — who was convicted of second-degree unintentional murder, third-degree murder and second-degree manslaughter on April 20, 2021 — to let him breathe.

I watched coast-to-coast and international protests in reaction to the broad-daylight murder of Floyd in particular and police violence against Black people in general. Watching looting and burning. Reading former President Donald Trump's tweet, "Any difficulty and we will assume control but, when the looting starts, the shooting starts." That tweet reminded me of former Mayor Richard J. Daley's order to "shoot to kill" any arsonists and to "shoot to maim or cripple" any looters in the wake of the urban uprising on the West Side of Chicago following Dr. King's assassination in 1968.

Watching TV reporters working their way through the crowd of protesters, snagging interviews while gagging from tear gas and watching young Americans cuffed and arrested, the lights, the action and the cameras was a sight all too familiar to me. I couldn't smell the tear gas, but I knew how much it burned the eyes. I wasn't struck by a nightstick but I knew the pain. I sat safely in my Chicago home, sheltered in place during a global COVID-19 pandemic, but I knew the apprehension.

All that I saw took me back more than half a century to the time when I was not a distant viewer but an on-the-scene witness. Back then, Rev. Martin Luther King, Jr. was assassinated on April 4, 1968, just five days after President Lyndon Baines Johnson announced he would not seek reelection. Two months later, Sen. Robert Kennedy was gunned down in California while campaigning for the Democratic Party nomination for president.

That August of 1968, I was a summer intern for *Newsweek* magazine, covering the anti-war protests in Chicago during the Democratic National Convention. As part of Newsweek's riot coverage team, I was partnered with John Culhane, one of the magazine's Chicago bureau correspondents. The two of us had been dropped off on the corner of Clark and LaSalle to cover the demonstrators.

Days earlier, Abbie Hoffman, one of the leaders of the Youth International Party, a.k.a. the Yippies, who reveled in freaking out the establishment, held a press conference announcing that he was going to dump LSD in Chicago's water supply.

Mayor Daley ordered Police Superintendent James Conlisk to get his men suited up and ready to do battle.

Five thousand peace activists were camped out in the area near the Lincoln Park Zoo. Just across Cannon Drive, Supt. Conlisk had thousands of police officers in full riot gear. Shortly before midnight, a police bullhorn commanded the hippies and the yippies to disperse. Not long after that, I saw an object fly from the mob of protesters into the assembly of police.

That's when all hell broke loose. Within minutes, Culhane and I saw swarms of people streaming south on the west side of Clark Street. They all looked panicked. Some had blood running down their faces. Culhane and I ran against the battered crowd to see just what was going on. We only got a few hundred feet before we saw what it was and it wasn't pretty. The police were clubbing anyone and everyone who wasn't wearing a blue uniform. Hugh Hefner, whose Playboy Mansion was only a few blocks away, was swatted on his ass by police. Culhane and I took shelter in the gated front yard of Hermon Baptist, the oldest African-American church on the North Side.

One of the policemen yelled, "walk to us." Culhane and I were wearing blue riot helmets that *Newsweek* had commandeered from the Detroit police to protect us from the rioters. We were in suits and ties with Chicago Police Department (CPD)-issued press credentials hanging around our necks. Culhane shouted "press, press." Another policeman yelled, "Come out of there motherf*ckers."

Before we cleared the churchyard, they began beating us with their night sticks. Although I had grown up in a blue-collar neighborhood a block and a half from Gary's Delaney projects in Indiana, this was the first — and only — time I've felt the sting of a billy club. Our helmets absorbed the blows to our heads but our backs and thighs were not as fortunate. The police had formed a shoulder-to-shoulder gauntlet along the street and we found ourselves immediately in a crush of people who were being

Donald J. Trump
@realdonaldtrump

ANY DIFFICULTY AND WE WILL ASSUME CONTROL BUT, WHEN THE LOOTING STARTS, THE SHOOTING STARTS.

bludgeoned from one cop to the next all the way south to the LaSalle Drive. I'd always thought of myself as a humane, caring person, but as I experienced one whack after the next, I quickly started twisting my body so that someone else was between me and the wildly swinging nightsticks.

After having beat us back to the corner of Clark and LaSalle, the baton-happy cops were done with us. We immediately got on a pay phone to call *Newsweek's* makeshift headquarters to report what we had experienced and endured. A *Newsweek* courier picked us up in a rental car and brought us back to headquarters.

Assuming that we had somehow provoked the police, Culhane and I were taken off of street duty and forced to stay in the office and work the telephones Monday night. The CPD's intentional beating of the press continued on the city's streets and in the parks.

By Tuesday night, Culhane and I were back out there, chasing cops who were chasing anti-war protesters. What had been a demonstration with thousands of Chicago police and National Guardsmen and other lawmen turned into a pitched battle with anti-war protesters from Grant Park to Lincoln Park.

When the four days and nights had ended, according to *The Guardian*, a total of 192 police officers were injured. One hundred and ten demonstrators went to the hospital, 668 people had been arrested, 425 demonstrators were treated at temporary

medical facilities, 200 were treated on the spot and 400 were given first aid for tear gas exposure.

While I have the distinction of being one of the first reporters beaten by the Chicago police during the 1968 Democratic National Convention, I was hardly the only one. There have also been more than one reporter hurt in the ongoing Black Lives Matter protests. Journalists covering those demonstrations have been tear gassed, hit by rubber bullets and ended up on the wrong end of a policeman's nightstick.

What we're going through today are protests and riots because of the police acting as if Black lives don't matter. Years ago, the anti-war protesters chanted, "the whole world is watching."

The Black Lives Matter protesters have been repeating that same chant. But this time, the whole world is joining in the protests.

Monroe Anderson holding a photo of himself, donning a helmet, in 1968 while covering the anti-war protests
Photo by Darius Griffin/*The TRiiBE*

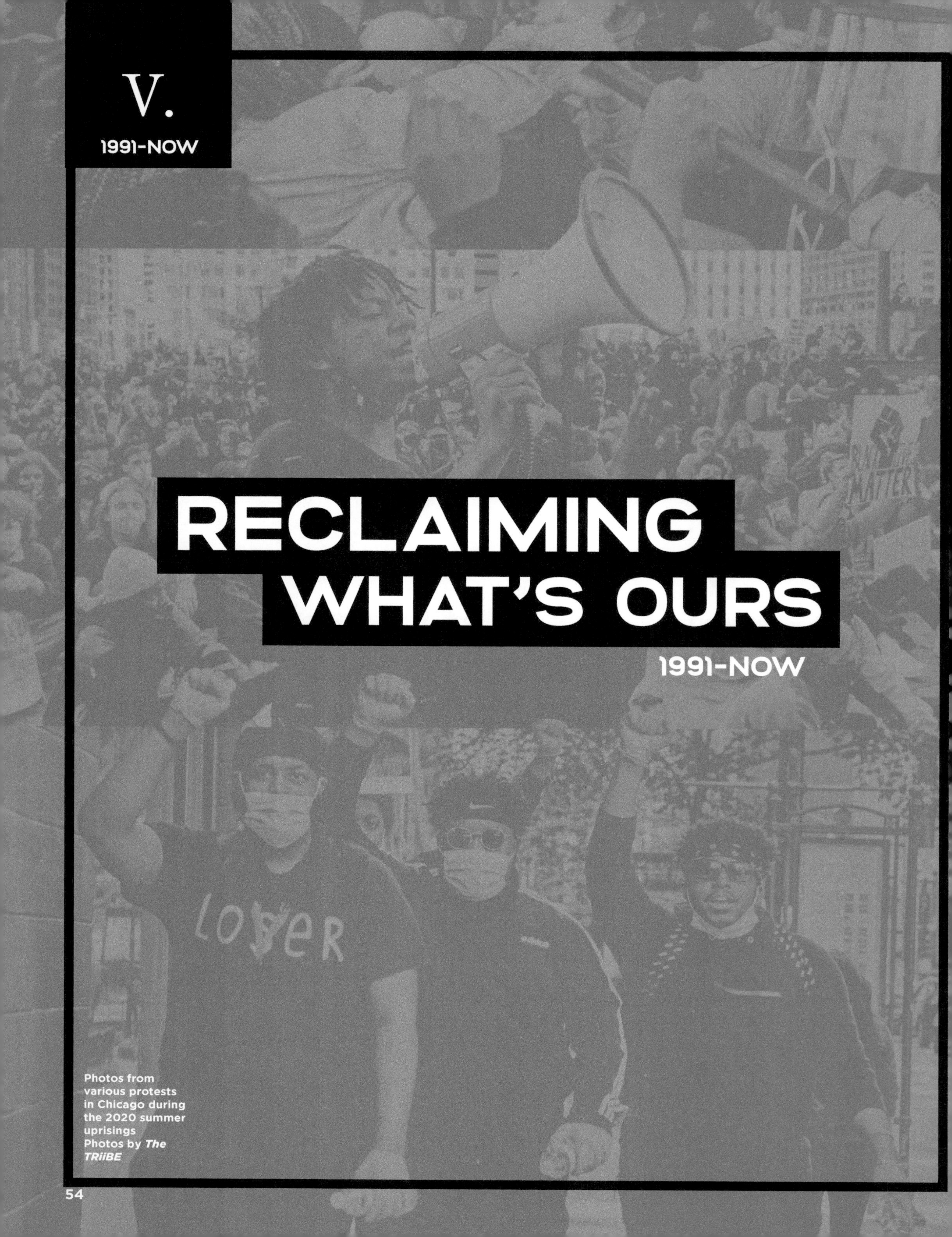

RECLAIMING WHAT'S OURS

1991-NOW

Photos from
various protests
in Chicago during
the 2020 summer
uprisings
Photos by *The
TRiiBE*

On Jan. 14, 2022, hundreds of CPS students walked out of their classrooms and marched onto CPS headquarters downtown in protest of the decision to return to in-person instruction amidst a local and national surge in COVID-19 omicron variant cases. Photo by Ash Lane/

"I AM A REVOLUTIONARY"

"I AM A REVOLUTIONARY" mural celebrating Illinois Black Panther Party chapter Deputy Chairman Fred Hampton, Mark Clark, and others at California and Madison.

Emmett Till and his mother Mamie lived in are memorialized on the Woodlawn home where they once lived; the home gained landmark status in 2021.

EBENEZER M.B. CHURCH
MISSIONARY BAPTIST
CHURCH
WELCOME

Gospel music was popularized by members of the Ebeneezer Missionary Baptist Church choir in the 1930s; the church, at 4501 S. Vincennes, was added to the National Register of Historic Places in 2016.

IN CHICAGO, BLACK HISTORY IS EVERYWHERE

BY NATALIE FRAZIER

It's often said that history—which adopts the form of landmarks, plaques and statues—is written by the victors. Black Chicago has a storied legacy of hard-fought victories, and in many cases it's been community members, family, and people from around the world who have done the work of commemorating them. They've done so by creating art, starting petitions to get landmark status, and raising funds to preserve historic sites as museums.

Cementing Black history in Chicago has historically taken many forms. Family members with no access to capital have pushed legislators to make homes into museums. For example, Fred Hampton Jr., Iberia Hampton, and the Save The Hampton House initiative fought for years to get the Maywood Village Board to recognize the childhood home of slain Black Panther leader Fred Hampton as a landmark. Sandra Cooper the great-granddaughter of Muddy Waters, collaborated with community organizations to obtain landmark status and funds to create the Mojo Museum. The Mojo Museum is located inside the first home Waters purchased, and it served as a gathering place for blues musicians and entertainers.

The home of *Chicago Defender* founder Robert S. Abbott, 4742 South Dr. Martin Luther King Jr. Drive, was added to the National Register of Historic Places in 1976.

The Ida B. Wells-Barnett House, where the trailblazing Black journalist lived in Bronzeville, is a national historic landmark.

THE HAMPTON HOUSE

FEED EM ALL

THE PEOPLES COMMUNITY FRIDGE

Illinois Black Panther Party Deputy Chairman Fred Hampton's childhood home in Maywood, IL, serves as a community resource hub

Honoring Black history has also meant protecting historic buildings from demolition. In March 2023, Preservation Chicago launched a petition to help The Warehouse, the birthplace of house music and the old stomping ground of a vibrant, Black, gay community, achieve landmark status. Over 14,200 people from all over the world have signed the petition and, in June, the Chicago City Council approved a landmark designation for it.

In the absence of ownership of a physical space, the community has found alternative ways to fortify the legacies of beloved Black figures. Although the Ida B. Wells Homes were demolished from 2002 to 2011, siblings Michelle Duster and Daniel Duster spent years lobbying local officials and raising funds for a commemorative sculpture honoring their great-grandmother. The "Light of Truth" monument honoring Ida B. Wells was finally erected in 2021.

The Black Panther mural at the corner of California and Madison which honors Fred Hampton Jr. and Mark Clark is another example of commemoration in the absence of a building.

In Chicago, history is everywhere. Buildings that stretch towards the clouds, massive statues, street names, murals, and museums honor myriad historical figures. Black history, however, might require a bit of a detour to find.

In unassuming two-flats on Lawrence and Lake Park, exterior walls of liquor stores on the West Side, and cul-de-sacs behind newly developed housing complexes near the lakefront, one can find the stories of revolutionaries, iconic DJs, and suffragettes. The heroes of Black Chicago have historically been ordinary people, so it is incredibly fitting that ordinary Black Chicagoans are shepherding the movements to honor them.

Photos by Ash Lane/*The TRiiBE*

"The Light of Truth," a monument to trailblazing Black journalist Ida B. Wells, was erected after years of efforts by her descendant Michelle Duster.

The Warehouse, an iconic club that was the birthplace of Chicago house music, was located in this building at 206 South Jefferson.

DAWGS
877-883-2947

Efforts are underway to turn blues legend Muddy Waters' former home at 4339 S. Lake Park into a "MOJO" Museum.

At a #CopsOutCps rally outside of CPS headquarters c Aug. 26, people occupied the street: footworking, juki bobbing, cupid shuffling and el caballo dorado. Photo Alexander Gouletas/*The TRiiBE*

WHEN REPORTING ON MOVEMENT ACTIONS, REVOLUTIONARY JOY MUST BE GIVEN THE SAME SPACE AS THE STRUGGLE

BY MATT HARVEY

Originally published in August 2020

At a vigil for Black lives on Aug. 26, 2020, organizers asked news crews standing front and center to move out of the way. "Mainstream media, this isn't your show," said Jae Rice of the Brave Space Alliance. "You don't have to leave, but moving a few feet back seems to be the most respectful thing to do right now."

This echoed sentiments shared by Jalen Kobayashi, an organizer with GoodKids MadCity just a few days before on Aug. 22, 2020 at the #BreakThePiggyBank protest.

"At large, you have done an absolutely abysmal, appalling job at covering what's going on in this city," Kobayashi said to cameras from WGN 9, CBS 2, ABC 7 and Univision.

While Kobayashi's speech is available online, it didn't make the nightly newscast for any of these channels. "I see too much coverage of looting and gun violence. You are not showcasing that we are having revolutionary joy," he continued.

On Aug. 26, 2020, two demonstrations

occurred as part of the movement to protect Black lives and defund the police. The first was a #CopsOutCPS rally outside of Chicago Public Schools (CPS) headquarters downtown during the hearing to decide the fate of the School Resource Officer (SRO) program in CPS.

Around 10:30 a.m., demonstrators gathered outside of CPS headquarters at the same time the Chicago Board of Education met to consider renewing an amended Chicago Police Department (CPD) contract for the SRO program and an accompanying resolution.

The board approved a one-year CPD contract, but cut the SRO program budget from $33 million to $12.1 million and increased scrutiny in SRO selection, including giving school principals the option to interview and select from officers trained to interact with students from marginalized communities and deemed eligible for SRO duty by CPD's Chief of Bureau Operations.

Meanwhile, a resolution was passed to require CPS to develop an

alternative plan to ensure safe school environments.

More than 100 demonstrators flooded the street outside of the CPS building's main entrance in a scattered semi-circle holding maroon signs that read, "#PoliceFreeSchools NOW."

Surrounding demonstrators were multiple news camera crews. Snacks, water, masks and other essentials were being lined up against the elevated bus stop as DJ iLLEST had already started hyping the crowd with his set, playing songs from artists like Chief Keef, DJ Nate, Tha Pope, Chance the Rapper and more.

My first thought was that the scene mirrored a block party as much as a protest. Then, Jennifer Nava of Brighton Park Neighborhood Council (BPNC) began with an opening statement.

"We have shared our stories, shown the stats, we have marched, rallied, gotten arrested, we've even shown up to some of your houses," she said. "You have deliberately chosen to ignore us, deny our truth, our experiences and our pain."

In an impassioned speech about the struggles of fighting for the safety of Black and brown students, Nava asserted the importance of revolutionary joy.

"Celebrating ourselves is a part of protest," she added. "Part of revolution is joy!"

That sentence set the tone for the rest of the action — a reminder that perhaps a protest that centers dance and music can be as potent an act of revolution as one that ends in police arresting demonstrators and issuing a curfew. Perhaps even more so.

After Nava spoke, people occupied the street: footworking, juking, bobbing, cupid shuffling and dancing el caballo dorado.

By the time protesters break for pizza around an hour in, the local news cameras have vanished — except for a lone cameraman from ABC 7— which is conveniently about a five-minute walk from the site of the demonstration. Besides independent photographers, I am the only reporter left to tell whatever is left of the story of this action— an action with minimal police presence and no confrontation.

However, at #BreakThePiggyBank, and other more tense demonstrations, cameras and reporters are there from beginning to end, documenting potential police confrontations as closely as they can.

When uprisings began Memorial Day weekend 2020, I recall being one of a few reporters in between police and protesters recording the demonstration on Wabash bridge, but being the only one out of many

reporters standing outside the broken windows of Nike Chicago who wasn't recording people leaving the scene with merchandise.

Organizers have deemed many outlets' protest coverage as untrustworthy because at best it falls short of capturing the totality of demonstrations, and actively presents protesters as nefarious actors at worst.

After the board vote, there is a clear sense of disappointment mixed with a general feeling of preparedness for this outcome. But even after more than six hours of protesting and waiting for this unsatisfying verdict, the joy hasn't been drained from the demonstrators, and speeches and chants start back up after the vote is over.

The second demonstration was a

Photo by Darius Griffin/*The TRiiBE*

candlelight vigil in Union Park to commemorate the casualties of the fight for Black lives, including Jacob Blake, who police in Kenosha, Wisc., shot seven times in the back a few days earlier, paralyzing him from the waist down. These demonstrations emphasized the value of what Kobayashi called "revolutionary joy," as well as the distrust organizers have for media outlets' ability to accurately portray their actions to their audiences.

When I arrive at Union Park around 8:00 p.m. for the vigil, a crowd of more than 200 is gathered around a baseball diamond. Candles are lit beneath the bench just outside the diamond and a cardboard sign leans against them with the message, "We stand with Kenosha."

As I walk closer to the diamond—the pulpit for the evening—I notice news vans packing up their equipment and heading out after organizers told them to back out of the middle of the gathering. Jae Rice, who uses they/them pronouns, is from Evanston, and has ties to Jacob Blake dating back to high school. Rice emphasized Blake's character from knowing him personally. "Back in high school, he was definitely a jokester," they reminisced.

The program carries on with speeches from activists from BYP 100, BLM Chi, and more, and performances from Black artists. One of the last performers is Kwirabura Intwari of the band Dcolonization, who begins with a song called "Hate," detailing the anger and exhaustion brought on by the constant fight for Black lives. He follows it with another song called "Dreams," that he opens by saying "I don't have anything else radical right now, so I'll do a love song because you are all lovely people."

The air is much heavier than what I witnessed outside of CPS, but the fight is no different.

"Some of the cops that were involved in Jake's shooting, or attempted lynching, were resource officers in schools," Rice said. "I need someone to give [Mayor] Lori Lightfoot the message that her well wishes for justice in regards to the Jacob Blake shooting doesn't mean shit when her unelected school board just voted to keep their contract with CPD."

As the evening ends and the crowd dissolves, the candles for the victims of police violence remain lit. I notice that the news cameras are long gone, and I can't help but recall Rice's request for them to back up, and Kobayashi's disdain for their trends in coverage.

Perhaps, if they'd been more willing to stay out in the morning to cover the revolutionary displays of joy expressed outside of CPS, they'd be more welcome during displays of revolutionary vulnerability.

On May 19, 2021, *The TRiiBE* had a one-on interview with Mayor Lori Lightfoot. Phot Ash Lane/*The TR*

THE REVOLUTIONARY COLUMN

AN ABOLITIONIST'S MIDTERM CONVERSATION WITH MAYOR LORI LIGHTFOOT BY BELLA BAHHS *Originally published in spring 2021*

"The Revolutionary Column," a series by raptivist Bella BAHHS where she spits revolutionary commentary on politics and pop culture.

It's May 19, the day before Mayor Lori E. Lightfoot's midterm anniversary in office, and each one of her press rooms on the 5th floor of City Hall are filled with journalists of color.

Back in 2016, Lightfoot presided over monthly Chicago Police Board hearings that I disrupted as a youth protester demanding that the board hold then-Chicago Police Department (CPD) Officer Dante Servin accountable for the 2012 murder of 22-year-old Rekia Boyd in North Lawndale.

I was co-organizing the budding Black youth-led prison abolition movement with the #LetUsBreathe Collective, Black Youth Project 100, Assata's Daughters and Black Lives Matter Chicago's Justice for Families working group.

I can't tell y'all how many times I've been in the same room with Lightfoot. But, she didn't seem to remember me — at least, if she did, she didn't let on.

Borrowing from one Black feminist organizer I admire and respect, Ella Baker, early in the interview I asked Lightfoot: "Who are your people? Who are you accountable to in this world — before and beyond being Chicago's mayor?" Lightfoot has worked for two anti-Black Chicago mayors— Richard M. Daley and Rahm Emanuel— that Black community leaders have been organizing against for decades.

"Who am I accountable to? I'm accountable to my heritage," she

said. "I'm accountable to the sacrifice that my parents made to put me in a position that I could succeed beyond their wildest expectations and dreams for themselves. I'm accountable to the people who elected me, who wanted to see something different, who felt like the status quo."

I'd hoped our first Black woman mayor would have mentioned the Black and brown Chicagoans who have been subjected to redlining and government-sanctioned anti-Blackness, and how those issues shaped the lives of many Black people whose families migrated from the South only to discover there was no refuge from racial violence here either. Since the Great Migration, many Black Chicago families have continued to struggle with housing and job discrimination, school segregation, fascist police and more.

Lori Lightfoot doesn't come from the same world that many Black Chicagoans like me did. She grew up in the small town of Massillon, Ohio, 50 miles south of Cleveland. She was raised in a predominantly white community, attending well-resourced, predominately white schools throughout her life. When she was class president in high school, one of the biggest issues she and her peers faced was bland cafeteria food.

I came to the interview wanting to get to the nitty-gritty: On national news outlets, Lightfoot has presented herself as a truly progressive Black queer woman mayor. But I specifically wanted to know more about her understanding of Black liberation

movements and the demands within them.

When I asked her which Black Chicago liberation struggle resonated most with her, she didn't mention any of the Black queer-led movements to end criminalization of Black LGBTOIA people and dismantle systems that perpetuate institutional racism and intersectional oppression. Instead, she told me about her brother Brian Lightfoot's 17-year stint in a federal prison for possession of and intent to distribute crack cocaine.

"I know he came out of that experience traumatized, because he didn't get access to good health care," Lightfoot said. "He didn't get access to the kind of job training and skills that he needed. And he didn't get access to a transition plan so that when he came out, he'd actually be able to land on his feet and not recidivate. He didn't get access to addiction counseling and support that he needed to keep him away from narcotics. So that's something very near and dear to me."

I asked what she's doing to help the ever-growing population of Black Chicagoans faced with post-conviction struggles. In a couple of weeks, she said, her administration will make an official announcement about new programs to support returning citizens.

Black low-income neighborhoods on the South and West sides have been hit hard by mass incarceration. The North Lawndale Employment Network estimates that more than

"IF YOU UNARM THE CITY WITH VALID DEFENSES AND OFFICERS, I THINK THE CONSEQUENCES ARE GOING TO BE MONUMENTAL.

70 percent of all North Lawndale men between the ages of 18 and 45 have criminal records. Although the state spends more than $1 billion annually to incarcerate Black and brown Chicagoans, there's been comparatively very little investment in reentry services.

"What I ideally would like to see coming out of IDOC, coming out of Cook County, is a real transition plan," Lightfoot continued. "We know when inmates are going to be released. Let's start six months ahead of time, if not sooner, in talking to them about the things that they need to know: how to be connected to services, whether it's Medicaid, whether it's food stamps [or] job training."

In March, when Fox News asked Lightfoot about the backlog of cases in the criminal courts, she said, "We've arrested literally thousands of people who have been involved in car thefts, carjackings and so forth, but what happens is within 24 or 48 hours, they're back out on the street and the backlog of criminal cases isn't moving, because Cook County hasn't figured out that they can actually do criminal trials virtually like Lake County."

Now we all know what Fox News is about. In a 2019 interview with "The Breakfast Club" radio show, former Fox News host Eboni Williams said the network was founded for the sole purpose of "the demonizing of the other." Mayor Lightfoot skillfully panders to different audiences like a true politician. During our interview, she said nothing about arresting carjackers or keeping criminals locked up when discussing this topic.

Instead, she offered this: "When people get arrested, and they have a charge hanging over their head, and their case isn't moving, what we've seen — and there's been a number of studies in Cook County about

this — [is] people end up pleading guilty because they just wanted to be done." she told me. "If you're not guilty of something, under our Constitution, you have to have your day in court. And with the criminal courts not being open, and cases not moving, people aren't getting their day in court."

Naturally, that brought us to Cook County State's Attorney Kim Foxx. In her first two years in office, nearly 4,500 fewer felony retail theft charges were filed as a result of her raising the threshold for approving felony charges to $1,000 from $300. And though I wouldn't go so far as to call Foxx an abolitionist, she has certainly been a leader in bond reforms that have gotten us closer to abolition. In February, Illinois became the first state in the nation to end money bail. I wanted to know how Lightfoot feels about the movement to decarcerate Chicago.

"I don't think Cook County Jail should be a debtors' prison, and that's a big part of, I think, things that Kim has talked about," Lightfoot began. "But I want to also say we can't forget the victims. I was just on a Zoom on Saturday with a number of mothers whose children had been killed by gun violence in the city. Their pain was just pouring through the screen. What they feel like is there's nobody there for them."

While families impacted by gun violence may feel temporary satisfaction when a perpetrator of harm is arrested, tried and convicted, that is not justice.

The criminal legal system is not equipped to heal the families

of victims of gun violence, who also have very little say in how criminal proceedings are handled. The way Mayor Lightfoot equates accountability with carceral punishment is troubling for Black Chicago.

Even more troubling is the disparity in what she believes accountability looks like for police officers. Sparked by the murder of George Floyd, Black revolutionaries in Chicago were protesting everyday for months in 2020. I asked Mayor Lightfoot what her views are on the proposed George Floyd Justice in Policing Act, which aims to eliminate qualified immunity, a policy that helps police officers escape legal liability for civil rights violations. Her response revealed how disconnected she is from Chicago's Black liberation movement.

"If you unarm the city with valid defenses and officers, I think the consequences are going to be monumental. I think the amount of money that we are paying out in settlements and judgements is only going to go up exponentially," she said. "I think, as an officer, if you believe that you've made an honest mistake, and you're now going to risk your pension, your salary, your house, your future, I don't know who would take that job."

By this point, revolutionaries, I was livid. I wanted to walk out of the press room. I couldn't believe that she was sitting in my face telling me that we should not abolish qualified immunity because it will make policing a less attractive job. But I had an interview to finish.

Bella BAHHS interviews Mayor Lightfoot. Photo by Ash Lane/*The TRiiBE*

V. RECLAIMING WHAT'S OURS

1991–PRESENT

BY MATT HARVEY

From the time Black folks started building communities in Chicago in the 19th century, there has been an endless struggle to protect those communities from the scourge of white supremacy. Black codes, labor discrimination, redlining, gentrification, underinvestment and over-policing are all ways that institutionalized racism has attempted to thwart the prosperity of Black people in Chicago. In the late 20th century, the dominant narratives of Black Chicago (and Black America at-large) are contrasting ones. In one, Black communities are wrought with widespread poverty due to de-industrialization, and crime due to white supremacist intervention. The other narrative is of Black heroes — individuals whose personal achievements are celebrated as proof of monumental Black progress.

Although Black people became the largest racial group in Chicago in 1990, the population steadily declined through that decade and into the present, initially due to the de-industrialization of the city's economy, and later the demolition of public housing and gentrification of neighborhoods where Black people were once a majority. Now, the future of Black Chicago is working to re-instill the prosperity once enjoyed by our grandparents and great-grandparents who thrived in the Black Metropolis. Through politics, activism, art and culture; this timeline is about reclaiming what's ours.

1990

The Chosen Few DJs collective, founded in the late 1970s by Wayne Williams, Jesse Saunders, Alan King, Tony Hatchett, and Andre Hatchett, threw its first reunion picnic and house celebration in Jackson Park in 1990. They continued the tradition the following year, and the Chosen Few DJs Picnic & House Music Festival has since grown into a yearly event that draws tens of thousands of house heads.

Scenes of residents of Stateway Gardens and Cabrini Green housing projects, Chicago, Illinois.

1992

Dr. Mae Jemison, a graduate of Morgan Park High School on Chicago's South Side, became the first Black woman to travel in space when she served aboard the Space Shuttle *Endeavor*. Jemison, who earned a medical degree at Cornell University, practiced medicine in Liberia and Sierra Leone before joining NASA.

1993

South Side native Carol Moseley Braun is the definition of a trailblazer. In 1993, she took office as the first African American woman elected to the U.S. Senate, the first African American U.S. Senator from the Democratic Party, the first woman to defeat an incumbent U.S. Senator in an election and the first female U.S. Senator from Illinois.

Carol Moseley Braun campaigns for a seat in the United States Senate, at the State of Illinois Center, 100 West Randolph Street, Chicago,

1995

Chicago experienced the most deadly environmental disaster in its history in July 1995 when a five-day heat wave led to the deaths of 739 people. Over 70% of the victims were elderly, most of whom were poor and couldn't afford air conditioning. Black people fell victim to the heat at a rate one-and-a-half times higher than white people. The tragedy shed light on the reality of environmental racism.

1996

In 1996, Barack Obama, a South Side community organizer and attorney, was elected to the Illinois state Senate representing the 13th District, which included the Hyde Park, Kenwood, South Shore, Chicago Lawn neighborhoods. In 2004, he was elected to the U.S. Senate. In 2008, he was elected the first Black president of the United States, giving his acceptance speech in front of thousands gathered at Grant Park.

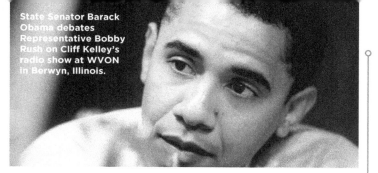

State Senator Barack Obama debates Representative Bobby Rush on Cliff Kelley's radio show at WVON in Berwyn, Illinois.

1998

Over Juneteenth weekend, nearly 3,000 people from around the country came to Chicago to participate in the founding convention of the Black Radical Congress (BRC). The BRC was first conceived by a group of five Black scholars and activists— Abdul Alkalimat, Bill Fletcher, Jr., Manning Marable, Leith Mullings, and Barbara Ransby—who had determined that Black radicals in America had a responsibility to address the state of social and political affairs regarding Black people.

2006

On December 9, 2006 Joan E. Higginbotham became the third Black woman in space when she worked aboard the Space Shuttle *Discovery* (STS-116) for 12 days. Higginbotham is an electrical engineer who was born and raised in Chicago. She retired from NASA in 2007 as a decorated astronaut having been awarded NASA's Exceptional Service Medal and the Adler Planetarium's Women in Space Science Award.

2007

In 2007, the last of the Robert Taylor Homes and the Stateway Gardens projects were demolished, finishing a radical reduction of public housing begun by the Chicago Housing Authority in the late 1990s. The two CHA housing projects once housed over 30,000 people combined and included some of the poorest U.S. census areas. The demolition was part of the CHA Plan for Transformation, which sought to replace the dilapidated low-income high-rises with low-rise mixed-income properties.

2012

In 2012, 16-year-old rapper Chief Keef released his second mixtape, *Back From the Dead*, featuring the hit single "I Don't Like." The song was an instant hit in Chicago and quickly went viral online. The attention Keef brought to Chicago reinvigorated the local music industry and catapulted drill music, a hip-hop genre invented in the city, to international acclaim.

2016

In 2016, after a decades-long fight for justice, 57 torture survivors were awarded $5.5 million in reparations for having suffered extreme abuse at the hands of former Chicago Police Department commander Jon Burge and the officers under his command from the 1970s to early 90s.

2018

Following nearly four years of intense protests and cries for justice in the murder of 17-year-old Laquan McDonald, in 2018 then-Chicago Police Officer Jason Van Dyke was convicted of second-degree murder and 16 counts of aggravated battery for the 2014 shooting, making him the first Chicago cop convicted of a murder committed while on duty in decades. In 2019, he was sentenced to six years and eight months in prison. He was released from prison in February 2022 after serving 39 months.

2010s: CHICAGO IS A HIP-HOP TRENDSETTER

The conversation around Chicago's musical influence is usually centered on blues, jazz, house, and R&B artists in the mid-20th century; but our contemporary creatives have been similarly influential throughout their music careers. Since the 1990s, Chicago has set trends in hip hop. Chance the Rapper, Kanye West and Chief Keef are now household names and are in part responsible for changing the music game in various ways. Prior to becoming a genre-redefining rapper-producer and fashion designer, Kanye was stirring soul into the tracks of local rappers like GLC, Twista and Consequence, and popping up at local cyphers in polos and backpacks. Before drill became hip-hop's most popping subgenre, Keef and his homies were crafting their influential sound on a computer with producer Young Chop. Chance's groundbreaking Grammy wins for a free mixtape were simply the outcome of a scaled-up version of the rapper handing out mixtapes at Chicago high schools. The talented rappers, songwriters and producers of Chicago's hip-hop scene have been the city's main cultural export.

Chance the Rapper, photo taken in 2022 by Ash Lane/*The TRiiBE*

2019

On April 2, 2019, after winning a runoff election against Cook County Board President Toni Preckwinkle, Lori Lightfoot made history by becoming the first Black woman and first openly gay person elected mayor of Chicago.

2020

Memorial Day Weekend 2020 marked the beginning of youth-led uprisings sparked by the murders of Breonna Taylor and George Floyd. In Chicago, the energy of that weekend carried on through the summer as organizers continued to fight against systemic racism in city institutions such as the Chicago Police Department, Chicago Public Schools and more.

2023

Fifty-five years to the day after Dr. Martin Luther King Jr., the moral architect of the Voting Rights Act, was assassinated in Memphis, and nearly 40 years after Harold Washington upset the Chicago machine to become the city's first Black mayor, Brandon Johnson—buoyed by overwhelming support in Black communities on the South and West Sides—defied the political establishment and won the April 4 runoff for Chicago mayor.

As Indigenous and Black communities navigate the politics of our settler state, our collective movements ground us to where we come from — the land. Photo by Darius Griffin /// The TRiiBE

WE MUST VIEW INDIGENOUS SOVEREIGNTY AS TANTAMOUNT TO BLACK LIBERATION

BY FAWN POCHEL   *Originally published in summe*

When the pandemic hit the United States in 2020, Chi-Nations Youth Council (CNYC) worked to redistribute nearly $10,000 into Chicago's Native community that spring.

Soon, CNYC shifted its focus from mutual aid to direct action. Chi-Nations helped organize the Black and Indigenous solidarity rally held on July 17 which led to the removal of three Christopher Columbus statues.

Since its founding in 2012, Chi-Nations has been advocating for the abolishment of Columbus Day alongside ongoing calls for the removal of racist monuments and mascots. As an auntie of CNYC, I was asked to help write the Indigenous Peoples' Day Ordinance submitted to Chicago's City Council by Ald. Rossana Rodriguez-Sanchez, the first Latinx alder to represent the 33rd Ward.

As the rally took place on unceded lands, people gathered at the center of Grant Park on 301 S. Columbus Drive. It was kicked off by performances and speakers, including Bobby Joe Smith III, a Black and Lakota artist and professor.

"Black and Indigenous folks are the most dangerous union to the stability of America because we know we are not Americans. We are older than America. We understand that the premise of America is our subjugation and erasure," Smith said to the growing crowd in the park. "That is why when others bemoan [of] strange and uncertain times, we see

[it] as an opportunity to tear down a system that has always been violently abnormal, amoral and unsustainable."

The relationship between Indigenous and Black people has always been complicated by the interference of white supremacy.

The United States government actively played a role in erasing the existence of Afro-Indigenous identity through the paper genocide of blood quantum enrollment — which requires a person to have a certain number of "full-blood" ancestors to be considered a member of an Indigenous tribe — and the "one-drop rule," which considered anyone with a single Black ancestor to be Black. Stolen land and stolen labor built this country.

The demand for justice within our settler-colonial systems is a call for immediate change and the abolishment of oppressive powers. Indigenous and Black movements toward collective liberation call into question the validity of the settler state that has targeted our communities. Indigenous and Black movements have always worked in relation to place. In order for there to be liberation on Anishinabek Land, Chicago, we must view Indigenous sovereignty as tantamount to Black liberation.

Over nearly 100 years, the U.S. ratified approximately 368 treaties with various Indigenous communities. And since 1871, the U.S. has violated every one it signed. At the foundation of American-Indian treaty-making was

this fundamental truth that tribes are independent nations that hold rights to self-determination.

But the very notion of Manifest Destiny — that American settlers were destined to expand across North America — was conceived to reinforce the ideology that western conquest was ordained by God to expand American imperialism.

Expansionism under Manifest Destiny upheld the belief in the natural superiority of the white/Anglo-Saxon race and justifies the appropriation of Indigenous land. These beliefs continue to support militant white nationalist identities while relegating Indigenous and Black people to the fringes of society.

As Indigenous and Black communities navigate the politics of our settler state, our collective movements ground us to where we come from — the land. The return to land-based practices must center the history of the land itself in order to strategically build community power toward the goals of rematriation and reparations.

With each broken treaty, Chicago transformed into the frontlines of colonial occupation and resistance.

"You say of us that we are treacherous, vindictive and cruel; in answer to the charge, we declare to all the world with our hands uplifted before high Heaven, that before the white man came upon us, we were kind, outspoken, and forgiving. Our real character has been misunderstood because we have

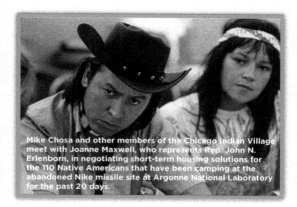
Mike Chosa and other members of the Chicago Indian Village meet with Joanne Maxwell, who represents Rep. John N. Erlenborn, in negotiating short-term housing solutions for the 110 Native Americans that have been camping at the abandoned Nike missile site at Argonne National Laboratory for the past 20 days.

resented the breaking of treaties made with the United States, as we honestly understood them," Simon Pokagan, an author, activist and member of the Pokagon Band of Potawatomi, wrote in 1833.

"Your own historians, and our traditions, show that for nearly 200 years, different Eastern powers were striving for mastery in the new world, and that our people were persuaded by the different factions to take the war-path, being generally led by white men who had been discharged from prisons for crimes committed in the Old World," he continued.

When the second Treaty of Chicago was signed in 1833, it granted the U.S. all lands west of Lake Michigan to Wisconsin's Lake Winnebago. In return, the treaty promised various cash payments and tracts of land west of the Mississippi River. Despite these promises, the U.S. government never paid for the lands it usurped.

"The only payment for land is land and we can't allow for [western] institutions to claim they do decolonizing work," said Adrien Pochel, co-founder of First Nations Garden, and my nephew. Currently, the First Nations Garden is the largest property within Chicago that is managed by Anishinabek and other First Nations peoples.

In urban areas such as Chicago, violence against Native people is invisibilized. Our existence is tokenized and historicized through performative acts such as President Joe Biden's proclamation to recognize May 5 as Missing and Murdered Indigenous Women (MMIW) Day without recognizing the state's role within the epidemic.

The epidemic of violence against Indigenous women isn't due to a

crack in the landscape of justice; rather, it's part of a calculated system that targets Native bodies that have been upheld throughout America's history of policing. Policing in this nation has never been about justice; it's about subjugation and erasure. The system is not failing; it is explicitly designed to protect the state against Indigenous and Black movements toward liberation.

We see the ongoing impact of Manifest Destiny today within the institutions that were designed to spread American values. The creation of such western institutions is rooted to racist ideologies that help the state maintain control of wealth and resources. In 1969, an activist group which would come to be known as the Chicago Indian Village (CIV) was formed as a result of poor living conditions and unethical eviction practices experienced by Native Americans in Chicago.

The group came together — erecting the Wrigleyville Protest Camp in 1971 — as a result of the eviction of Carol Warrington, a Menominee mother of six who staged a rent strike to demand her landlord remedy the poor upkeep of her rental property. Despite initially being in support of the protest camp, the American Indian Center INC (AIC) called for the occupation to disperse. As a nonprofit, AIC upholds its purpose of serving the state, restricting radical imaginations to ensure the path of least resistance.

While the CIV was short-lived, disbanding in 1972, the group successfully took over Chicago's Belmont Harbor for two weeks, demanding affordable housing for Native Americans, a school for Native youth and the redistribution of AIC's resources from social events toward acts of self-determination for Chicago's Native Community.

"All white men are the devil... The Black man is my brother... I'm rising up angry," activist Pee Wee Taylor told the Chicago Daily News during the Belmont Harbor occupation. A sentiment that is embedded in today's movements for collective liberation.

In 1972, Chicago's Little Big Horn

High School was opened as a result of Native organizing. "Little Big Horn was established to meet the needs of Indian students," Lucille St. Germaine, the school's coordinator, told the New York Times in 1976. "Five years ago, the dropout rate for American Indians was 95 percent in Chicago. Our dropout rate this year was 11 percent, so we must be meeting their needs."

More than 50 years after the CIV, a faction of the Chicago Native community still distrusts nonprofit organizations when it comes to social change. The slogan "Save a Community, Kill a Nonprofit" is sketched on a plywood board that is to be installed at the First Nations Garden. The piece will be part of an outdoor gallery we created with local artists to reflect on the relationship to land and community.

The Saulteaux artist Justice Marie, who is contributing her art to the space, explains that the slogan is meant to draw attention to how traditional nonprofits uphold a racist system by looking past moral and ethical concerns.

"They [AIC] have a defense lobbyist who is a part of the Chicago Police Department's Knights of Columbus. We no longer have the luxury to pretend nonprofits do right by us. We need to continue to make our own spaces and build from within the community instead of relying on governing bodies that uphold white supremacy," Marie said.

As a former member and employee of AIC, I have recently walked away from the organization in attempts to salvage my own morality. During the 2020 election, the American Indian Center installed an "All Life Matters" mural and has yet to address the organization's anti-Blackness.

Black and Indigenous futures are dependent on breaking free from the oppressions of dispossession and enslavement. The mechanisms and systems of white supremacy rely on disconnecting us from not only each other but the land itself. Therefore, calls for liberation must work to hold accountable all systems that have profited from white supremacy.

KIM FOXX BLAZED A TRAIL OF PROGRESSIVE REFORMS IN THE STATE'S ATTORNEY'S OFFICE

BY TONIA HILL & JIM DALEY

Cook County State's Attorney Kim Foxx. Photo by Ash Lane/*The TRiiBE*

On April 25, Cook County State's Attorney Kim Foxx announced during a speech at the City Club of Chicago that she would not seek reelection in 2024.

"At the conclusion of my term, November of 2024, I will be stepping down as State's Attorney. I will not be on next year's ballot, by my choice," Foxx told the room.

It's not a decision that she made lightly, she added.

"I became State's Attorney to deliver safety, justice and equity. I feel that I have made my mark, so I'm ready to let new leadership step forward," Foxx said in a written statement following the speech. "Over the next year and half, my office will continue to work diligently for the people of Cook County and uphold the values of a fair and just legal system."

Before Foxx's remarks, Cook County Board President Toni Preckwinkle, who Foxx worked under for two years, spoke at length about their work on criminal justice reforms and how Foxx continued that work when she became Cook County State's Attorney in 2016.

"She's led her office through one of the most turbulent and unprecedented times in recent history, with a global pandemic and a national surge in gun violence, which has profoundly impacted our local communities," Preckwinkle said. "During this time, she's focused on collaboration, community outreach, and transparency."

Foxx, who was raised by her mother and grandmother in the Chicago Housing Authority's Cabrini-Green project on the Near North Side, obtained her law degree at Southern Illinois University. A survivor of childhood sexual assault, she worked in the Cook County Public Guardian's Office before joining the Cook County State's Attorney Office (CCSAO), where she worked for 12 years as an Assistant State's Attorney. Preckwinkle hired Foxx as a deputy chief of staff in 2013 and later promoted her to chief of staff.

She was swept into office as a reform candidate in 2016, becoming the first Black woman to run the CCSAO. She won 58 percent of the vote in a three-way Democratic primary and 72 percent in the general election.

The Chicago Alliance Against Racism and Political Repression (CAARPR) praised Foxx for her "contributions to

the cause of justice" in a statement released on April 25. "The Chicago Police Department is so filled with racism, corruption and criminal behavior, it can only be swept clean by the power of a massive movement," the statement read in part. "The election of Kim Foxx in 2016 was an expression of the masses desire for justice as she received 1.5 million votes."

Anita Alvarez, the incumbent State's Attorney whom Foxx defeated in the 2016 primary, had been the target of an activist campaign to remove her from office following the murders of Rekia Boyd in 2012 and Ronald Johnson and Laquan McDonald in 2014, by Chicago police officers, and the SA's office failure to hold CDP to account.

"We were not there to say vote for this person or that [Foxx] is a person who's going to fix everything, because our position was that we were against the prosecutor's office, period," Aislinn Pulley told *The TRiiBE*. "But specifically, we needed to get Anita Alvarez out of the office."

Pulley is the executive director of the Chicago Torture Justice Center. She also founded the Chicago Black Lives Matter chapter in 2014 and was one of the organizers leading the "Bye Anita" campaign, which consisted of multiple organizations, including Assata's Daughters, BYP100, Fearless Leading By Youth (F.L.Y.), and more.

For Pulley, an abolitionist, and others centrally involved in the campaign, the SAO's office has a history of causing irreparable harm in Black and brown communities.

Foxx consistently acknowledged past harms the SA's office have carried out on marginalized groups, "I have to say, we have to go back to Fred Hampton and Mark Clark," Foxx said during her farewell announcement. Foxx referenced the murders of Black Panther leaders by CPD during her speech to a room full of her colleagues and other elected leaders.

Once in office, Foxx set out to institute reforms. She became a leader in the effort to reform cash bail, agreeing early in her tenure to release people arrested for nonviolent offenses who had bail set at amounts less than $1,000. The move was initially praised, but as she initiated additional reforms such as exonerating wrongfully convicted people, and as the push to abolish cash bail gained momentum, Foxx became the target of criticism by adherents to traditional tough-on-crime approaches.

But she pressed on with reforming the CCSAO. In 2018, Foxx had the office create an open data portal and released six years' worth of felony case data, the first of its kind in the country. Residents can enter their ZIP codes and find out how many arrests have been made, how many cases were referred to the CCSAO, how many people were charged, whether there were convictions and what type of sentence was given. Under Foxx, the CCSAO created roles such as the first-ever Chief Data Officer and Chief Diversity, Equity and Inclusion officer.

In 2019, she began expunging marijuana convictions, and by 2022 had surpassed 15,000 such expungements. She also directed CCSAO to stop prosecuting shoplifting under $1,000 and to dismiss drug cases in favor of alternatives to prosecution. Ultimately, Foxx declined to file charges in thousands of low-level cases that her predecessor would have prosecuted.

"SHE'S LED HER OFFICE THROUGH ONE OF THE MOST TURBULENT AND UNPRECEDENTED TIMES IN RECENT HISTORY.

Yet, Foxx gained national attention not from her reform efforts, but from controversy after the office dropped charges against Jussie Smollett in 2019. The actor was accused of staging an attack on himself in River North, and was arrested for filing a false police report.

Still, Foxx overcame relentless media coverage and criticism regarding her handling of the Smollett case and went on to win reelection with 54 percent of the vote in 2020.

During the 2020 rebellions in the wake of the police murder of George Floyd, Foxx issued a policy to decriminalize protest, making her one of the only prosecutors in the nation to do so.

Under her watch, the CCSAO has vacated 114 convictions tied to Ronald Watts, a former CPD sergeant who led a crew of corrupt cops in terrorizing residents of the Ida B. Wells housing project in Bronzeville. Watts, who extorted people, lied under oath and robbed drug dealers, was sentenced to 22 months in prison in 2013 after he pled guilty to robbing an undercover FBI officer.

Foxx also asked the court to vacate eight murder convictions tied to disgraced CPD detective Reynaldo Guevara, who has been the subject of multiple wrongful conviction lawsuits that have cost the city more than $70 million. She also expanded the CCSAO's Convictions Integrity Unit adding new positions specifically to scrutinize cases tied to disgraced CPD Commander Jon Burge.

By August 2022, Foxx had granted 229 exonerations. Largely as a result of her efforts, Illinois led the nation in exonerations from 2018 to 2021.

Foxx's work around bail reform, wrongful convictions, and exonerations can be applauded, Pulley said, because they've led to a reduction in incarceration and were important and historic.

"Many of the things that she was able to do were a part of beginning to reverse the policies that created the behemoth of incarceration that we have today, which is the most people incarcerated in the world," Pulley explained.

Though Foxx has made positive steps to reduce the footprint of incarceration, Pulley said there's still more work to be done. "The State's Attorney's Office needs to stop fighting torture survivors cases, defending torturous cops," Pulley added.

"I do this on behalf of those kids who are dying in our streets right now whose potential we are losing out on because of our failing policies," Foxx said. "It has been my honor and my privilege to represent them with the fullest, and in my next lifetime my advocacy for these issues will not waver."

Cook County State's Attorney Kim Foxx announced in a speech to the City Club on April 25 that she will not seek reelection in 2024. Photo by Ash Lane/ *The TRiiBE*

UNDERSTANDING POLICE AND PRISON ABOLITION: ACTIVISTS SAY REFORM IS NOT ENOUGH

BY MATT HARVEY   *Originally published in July 2020*

Since the May 26, 2020 uprising in Minneapolis that sparked nationwide civil unrest in response to the murders of George Floyd and Breonna Taylor, progressive ideals such as community control of policing and removal of police officers from schools have begun to permeate the mainstream. But these are baby steps in the direction of a more radical movement: abolition.

What abolition means today is as clear-cut as it was in the 19th century, when it literally meant ending the institution of slavery and freeing Black folks — and this article likely would have featured the voices of Harriet Tubman and Frederick Douglass. The contemporary abolition movement has simply replaced chattel slavery with police and prisons.

The unambiguous demand to remove resources from the police is rooted in the movement toward the abolishment of police and prisons.

In 2023, the Chicago Police Department (CPD) has a $1.94 billion budget. For numerous abolitionists in Chicago, the overarching idea is that society is endangered — not protected — by the current system, which 2019 mayoral candidate Amara Enyia described as "retributive rather than restorative."

Reform "smothers in the sense that it only half addresses the systemic problem of police violence against communities they are sworn to protect," she explained.

"We're spending tens of millions making sure there are police officers in the schools. Meanwhile many of these schools don't have access to libraries, nurses, or counselors," Enyia said. "These are the things that build stronger, more resilient kids. It's a concrete example of where we could take money that we're spending on policing and direct it towards resources that benefit the community."

The effort to remove CPD from Chicago schools is a blitz against the School-to-Prison Pipeline (SPP). The SPP is an analysis of the education system that has discovered that the proliferation of zero-tolerance policies in schools and students being arrested by officers, contributes to the disproportionate incarceration of Black kids.

According to the U.S. Department of Education's Office of Civil Rights, Black students are three to four times more likely to be suspended or expelled than white students, and nearly three times more likely to end up in juvenile detention.

"If you take a look at the origins of policing in America, you'll find that it stems directly from slavery where it began as a tool to terrorize Black and indigenous people," Enyia said.

"Day of Protest" in Chicago following the death of George Floyd in summer 2020. Photo by Darius Griffin/*The TRiiBE*

Within the abolitionist framework, police and prisons are inseparable.

West Side artist and self-proclaimed "raptivist" Bella Bahhs was confronted with the terrors of the prison industrial complex at an early age, when both her parents were incarcerated.

"This system saw it fitting to take my parents from me, so I grew up feeling like this wasn't the just way for us to be governed," she said.

"People often operate under this assumption that Black people are inherently violent and criminal, and without police, everything will devolve into chaos," Bahhs said. "I believe that Black people are perfectly capable of governing [their] own communities, and enforcing accountability amongst ourselves in a restorative way."

Bahhs pictures this as more than changing the law of the land, instead envisioning the creation of an entirely new Black American nation.

According to Enyia, the idea of defending the police and reallocating resources to other social welfare programs has already proven viable.

Take Sweden, for example, where mental health professionals are deployed without police accompaniment. And Scotland saw a 60% decrease in homicides after it began treating violence as a public health issue.

"I believe Black people and Indigenous people are owed reparations in the form of money, land, and essential resources," Bahhs said. "Within this nation we can build a framework that emphasizes restorative justice by investing in education, providing jobs and basic necessities."

So what then of societal infractions? How do abolitionists plan to deal with the inevitable scenario in which one individual wrongs another? Bahhs explains a system in which these situations are rectified in a way that teaches and truly reforms, and accountability is up to the community to decide.

Enyia gives the example of block club monitoring, and how the existing infrastructure of local block clubs can be propped up to give neighbors the ability to protect their own communities.

Abolition's diversity of thought shouldn't necessarily count against the movement, according to organizer Destiny Harris, a poet, Howard University sophomore, and abolitionist from the West Side.

"We just have to keep the fight going on the ground," they said. "The people at the forefront of this movement— who are mostly Black women and queer folks— are doing a great job of keeping the battle going."

On Tuesday, April 4, 2023, Chicago elected Brandon Johnson to be its next mayor. Photo by Tyger Ligon for The TRiiBE.

AS MAYOR, BRANDON JOHNSON IS INVITING YOU TO REIMAGINE SAFETY IN CHICAGO

BY TONIA HILL, JIM DALEY & TIFFANY WALDEN

Fifty-five years to the day after Dr. Martin Luther King Jr., the moral architect of the Voting Rights Act, was assassinated in Memphis, and 40 years after Harold Washington upset the Chicago machine to become the city's first Black mayor, Brandon Johnson—buoyed by overwhelming support in Black communities on the South and West Sides—defied the political establishment and won the April 4 runoff for mayor.

"It was right here in the city of Chicago, that Martin Luther King Jr. organized for justice, dreaming that one day that the civil rights movement and the labor rights movement will come together," Johnson said in his victory speech in the South Loop. "Well, Rev. Martin Luther King Jr., the civil rights movement and the labor rights movement have finally collided. We are experiencing the very dream of the greatest man who ever walked the earth."

Johnson narrowly won the April 4 runoff over former Chicago Public Schools (CPS) CEO Paul Vallas after receiving 52 percent of the vote, while Vallas received about 48 percent after all votes were counted. Johnson won all of the city's majority-Black wards.

Turnout was key to Johson's victory, and organizers from multiple labor unions, including the Chicago Teachers Union (CTU) and SEIU, and political organizations such as the Chicago Alliance Against Racism and Political Repression (CAARPR), helped get him over the finish line. United Working Families (UWF), an independent political organization, endorsed Johnson and canvassed on his behalf throughout the election cycle. Since January, UWF estimates that through its volunteer field program, they've knocked on half a million doors in Chicago and made a million phone calls.

Youth voter turnout played a significant role in Johnson's win. Voters aged 18 to 24 increased their turnout by about 5,000 votes on April 4 compared to February 28, an increase of more than 30 percent. Overall, the 18-to-24 age cohort accounted for nearly 4 percent of ballots cast on April 4.

"It will be a new day in Chicago in terms of progressive policies, and it might be a way for us to stop the exodus of African Americans from leaving the city of Chicago," said Delmarie Cobb, a veteran journalist and political consultant.

The seeds for Johnson's ascendance to City Hall's fifth floor were planted a decade ago. In 2013, after then-mayor Rahm Emanuel closed 50 schools (most of which were on the South and West Sides), then-CTU president Karen Lewis, of the union's Caucus of Rank and File Educators (CORE), determined that labor actions alone were not enough to advance the caucus's progressive agenda and protect neighborhood schools. They established a political action fund and began running candidates for local and downstate office. Johnson, a former teacher and longtime CORE organizer, was elected to the Cook County Board of Commissioners in 2018.

Now, Johnson is asking Chicagoans to do something that's been seemingly impossible for administration after administration, something that unequivocally knocks the status quo off its square. Something so ostensibly radical that it trips racial fault lines. Something that, if given room to breathe, could very well undermine the foundational notion that Black Americans are inherently inferior—that instead, if their communities are truly invested in, they will thrive.

Johnson is asking Chicagoans to reimagine public safety. It's been a persistent throughline of Black liberatory thought dating back at least to the first cries to abolish slavery, stretching onward to the 2020 unrest following the police killing of George Floyd—and beyond.

This reimagining challenges the notion that safety can only be reactive to violent crime, where a shooting happens and the police show up, for example. Instead, reimagining public safety requires a kind of world-building. What are the root causes that lead a person to commit that crime, and how can they be prevented?

"We'll have a mayor that will listen to the public, particularly poor people and young people because the past mayors we've had have not done that," said Robert Starks, a professor emeritus of Political Science at Northeastern Illinois University. "They've overlooked the children and the poor."

During a one-on-one interview with *The TRiiBE* on March 23, Johnson spoke about the ways in which his platform aligns with grassroots organizers, who for centuries have questioned whether the institution of policing actually protects Black people, and dreamed of reimagining the system.

"I think there's an assumption that calling the police budget into question means getting rid of police," Johnson said. "And I guess it just depends on who you ask, but the fear is how do you ask a system to protect you when the system has been used to brutalize you at the same time? That's the fear. Can a system that has historically brutalized also protect?"

Johnson added that the impetus for reforming the criminal legal system is deeply rooted in abuses perpetrated by law enforcement.

"Police brutality case after police brutality case, people begin to lose hope that it was possible to not only repair damages, but to hold the system accountable," he said. "The call to action was centered around young people's desire to see real justice [but] could not find it working through the system, and wanted to provoke a more sincere conversation about the role of policing in Black communities in particular."

Many of the progressive goals that Chicago organizers have been fighting for are the foundational world-building blocks of Johnson's campaign. He vowed to support Bring Chicago Home, which would increase the real estate transfer tax on real-estate sales valued over $1 million to create a dedicated revenue stream to address homelessness. He also vowed to create a homeless preference at the Chicago Housing Authority (CHA) to prioritize them for housing choice vouchers and site-based units.

He wants to immediately enact a freeze on the transfer of CHA land to non-housing uses. Such controversial land swaps have led to the construction of a new $150 million open-enrollment school near the South Loop, or the construction of Chicago Fire Football Club practice facility for professional soccer, instead of new housing promised to those forced out of public housing. In 2015, community organizers and residents from Dearborn, Ickes and Wentworth Gardens Homes called for city leaders to put a moratorium on CHA land transfers to create a plan for replacement housing, which was promised when the highrise project homes were demolished between the late 1990s and 2010s.

Additionally, Johnson vowed to double youth summer employment to over 60,000 jobs, reopen shuttered mental health clinics, support the Treatment Not Trauma ordinance to have health professionals, not police, respond to mental health crises, and promote 200 new police detectives to lower caseloads and improve murder clearance rates.

"It exists in every single institution, the structural violence that has been the prevailing form of governance," Johnson said. "And I believe that's why there's so much energy and excitement around my candidacy, because we made it very clear that the tale of two cities, we're going to put an end to that."

The crowd at Johnson's Election Night watch party brimmed with angst, excitement and pure Black joy as Johnson began pulling ahead of Vallas in the race.

"I'm glad that this is finally at an end. I'm hoping it comes to the correct conclusion. I believe that Brandon Johnson is the correct person for this job," said Sharyn Payne, a longtime Woodlawn resident and co-founder of Southside Organizing for Power (STOP).

About 2,000 people filled the Marriot Marquis in the South Loop, eagerly awaiting election results.

"THE CALL TO ACTION WAS CENTERED AROUND YOUNG PEOPLE'S DESIRE TO SEE REAL JUSTICE.

"If the numbers hold, that'll be great for Chicago. It gives us an opportunity to reset our path and figure out a different way of doing government in the city of Chicago, a way that supports our communities in a way that uplifts people and a way that addresses some of our nagging, long-standing challenges in the community and in the city," Ald. Pat Dowell (3rd Ward) told *The TRiiBE*.

By 9:00 pm, the energy in the room shifted to celebration mode as the 1992 house music classic "Percolator" began to flow out of the speakers. People all over the room began dancing in unison.

The energy in the room didn't dissipate. The room was still celebrating as Johnson took the stage to address the crowd after Vallas conceded.

"Chicago, tonight is just the beginning," Johnson told the crowd. "With our voices and our votes, we have ushered in a new chapter in the history of our city.

2023 Chicago Mayoral Runoff

Brandon Johnson won the April 4 runoff with 51.4% of the vote.

▮ Johnson ▮ Vallas

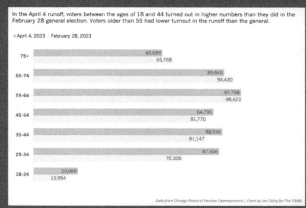

In the April 4 runoff, voters between the ages of 18 and 44 turned out in higher numbers than they did in the February 28 general election. Voters older than 55 had lower turnout in the runoff than the general.

■ April 4, 2023 ■ February 28, 2023

Age	April 4, 2023	February 28, 2023
75+	60,689	65,768
65-74	89,845	94,430
55-64	97,708	98,423
45-54	84,796	81,770
35-44	88,936	81,147
25-34	87,506	70,306
18-24	20,989	15,954

Data from Chicago Board of Election Commissioners | Chart by Jim Daley for The TRiiBE.

"The truth is the people have always worked for Chicago. Whether you wake up early to open the doors of your businesses, teach middle school or wear a badge to protect our streets or nurse patients in need or provide childcare services. You have always worked for this city. And now Chicago will begin to work for its people, all the people because tonight is a gateway to a new future for our city."

Throughout his speech, Johnson reiterated the heart of his campaign, which is to invest in people. He also added that he would build upon the legacy of Dr. Martin Luther King Jr., who brought his campaign to Chicago in the mid-1960s to shine a light on the inhumane living conditions for Black people on the West Side, and that of Chicago's first Black mayor, Harold Washington, who built a multi-racial coalition and enacted transformative change throughout his decades-long career in public life.

"Tonight is proof that by building a multicultural, multigenerational movement, we can bring together everyone. No matter if you live on the North, South, [or] West sides. We have demonstrated that we can change the world, Chicago. We finally will have a city government that truly belongs to the people of Chicago," he said.

That same evening, Lightfoot, in a written statement, congratulated Johnson on his win. "It is time for all of us as Chicagoans, regardless of our ZIP code or neighborhood, our race or ethnicity, the creator we worship, or who we love, to come together and recommit ourselves to uniting around our shared present and future. My entire team and I stand ready to collaborate throughout the transition period," the statement reads.

During a one-on-one interview with *The TRiiBE* on April 5, Johnson named public safety, public transportation, environment and housing as his top priorities.

He added that it's important to identify the people who can "unite our city around education, public safety, transportation, healthcare and environment," referring to people that will fill the roles in his administration's cabinet.

"I believe in co-governance. I want people to know that the process that I will lead will be transparent," Johnson said.

He said that during the first 100 days of his administration, he plans to address youth employment by doubling the number of young people hired for both summer and year-round positions. Johnson's inauguration took place May 15

In addition, Johnson wants to prioritize how the city handles mental health care services and wants to pass Treatment Not Trauma and Bring Chicago Home as well as conduct an impact study for the environment. He also plans to reopen the Department of Environment. The office was removed in 2011 under then-mayor Rahm Emanuel. Lightfoot created a new position in city government, the Chief Sustainability Officer, to replace the department.

Ald. Rossana Rodriguez-Sanchez (33rd Ward) first introduced the "Treatment Not Trauma" ordinance to the City Council's Health and Human Relations committee in 2020.

"I BELIEVE IN CO-GOVERNANCE.

As written, the ordinance would establish 24-hour crisis response teams within the Chicago Department of Public Health and deploy them citywide. The response teams would be equipped with a clinical social worker, emergency medical professional, or registered nurse.

Bring Chicago Home is a proposal that calls for restructuring the real-estate transfer tax on high-end property sales and imposing a one-time tax on sold properties; funds would be redirected toward efforts to combat homelessness.

"We cannot have people sleeping outside and I'm going to work very hard to see Bring Chicago Home become a reality," he said.

Johnson also wants to ensure that Chicagoans, even those that didn't vote for him, have a seat at the table. He said he is committed to uniting the city.

"Uniting this city in this moment is not just crucial and critical for the city of Chicago, but it's critical for our democracy because there's so much divisiveness," he explained. "I'm going to work hard every single day to continue to unite this city and I appreciate the opportunity to do that."

Brandon Johnson on Inauguration Day
Photo by Alexander Gouletas/*The TRiiBE*

IN BRANDON JOHNSON'S ADMINISTRATION, THERE'S OPPORTUNITY FOR BRAVERY

BY DAMON WILLIAMS
AS TOLD TO THE TRIIBE

When Brandon Johnson won the election to be Chicago's next mayor, my thoughts immediately went to 2020.

That May, following the police murder of George Floyd in Minneapolis, Chicago erupted in rebellions and demonstrations that the city responded to with brutality and increased surveillance of activists. I remember sitting in the Breathing Room on May 31, 2020 with a concussion and abrasions on my face from being slammed into the concrete by the Chicago Police Department (CPD) during a peaceful demonstration.

All that summer, a coalition was coming together. It was later named the Black Abolitionist Network, and it built the political community outreach campaign known as Defund CPD. At the time, organizer Asha Ransby-Sporn said that activists should make police investment a wedge issue that every mayoral and aldermanic candidate would have to answer to in 2023. And even five years before the 2020 rebellions, Ransby-Sporn named policy reforms such as body-worn cameras as being harm reduction, not transformative or abolitionist. That's significant, because Ransby-Sporn was the lead get-out-the-vote organizer on the South Side for Johnson's campaign.

And so the organizing that came out of the 2020 rebellions was one of the struggles for liberation that impacted the 2023 election. The Feb. 28 results of some aldermanic and police district council races, as well as Johnson making the runoff, showed the success of our organizing. Our political goals had already become a reality even before Johnson won the April 4 runoff.

I first met Brandon Johnson in 2016. At the time, Johnaé Strong and I were co-chairs of BYP100's Chicago chapter. After the release of the video of Laquan McDonald's murder by CPD officer Jason Van Dyke in 2015, our movement successfully toppled three targets: CPD Supt. McCarthy was fired; Cook County State's Attorney Anita Alvarez lost her reelection; and Rahm Emanuel decided not to run for mayor again. And so the movement gained legitimacy in the eyes of many, and particularly of folks who were in progressive politics, such as the Chicago Teachers Union (CTU).

Coming out of that, historian, professor and activist Barbara Ransby called together a coalition that would center the intersections of progressive elements of the labor movement and the burgeoning young Black radical movement. That was the first time we sat at tables with CTU, SEIU and UWF in an early grassroots collaboration for a big May Day action and one-day strike on May 1, 2016. I would say, in terms of the movement we have now and the coalition that's happening, I think that was the table

that started it. The action was robust. This is when Chicago State was at the risk of closing, and that then led to a feeder march that led to a huge demonstration downtown.

Soon after that, Page May, a phenomenal organizer, educator and movement builder, began getting harassed online by white racists for speaking up about resistance to police violence, and a number of the people targeting her were teachers. We realized that a lot of Chicago Public Schools (CPS) teachers are actually married to police officers.

As a result, Strong and I met with Stacy Davis Gates and Brandon Johnson. They were with about two or three other Black teachers who were basically the head of the informal Black Caucus in the CTU. They sat and struggled with us and were humble. They acknowledged the harm. They acknowledged the misalignment. They honored our work and our sacrifice and our dedication. They made a commitment to work with their people, and that it was important that we stay connected and that we build something together. And it is from that commitment that I think we are here today.

In many ways, that grassroots movement is what made this moment possible. Now, we must take care not to let that movement be erased.

I believe we have the opportunity for bravery. We have the opportunity for people to participate in revolution. That's because we have the opportunity now to repair, restore and transform which, if you expand those words, are reparations, restorative justice and transformation. Those are revolutionary approaches.

A get-out-the-vote rally hosted by New Mount Pilgrim's pastor, Rev. Marshall Elijah Hatch, Sr., and featuring 2023 mayoral candidate Brandon Johnson and Rev. Al Sharpton, a longtime civil rights leader. Photo by Ash Lane/*The TRiiBE*

How do we do that? We start by centering the harm that has been done to our communities. We also must organize collective accountability. And we must raise our own standards, raise our expectations and raise our ideals.

Once we center the harm we can acknowledge it, and that acknowledgement leads to accountability. Accountability allows us to heal. To do that, we have to hold those who have aligned with white supremacism accountable; we have to hold the new administration accountable; and we have to hold ourselves and the movement accountable.

What does it look like to center the harm, which is what restorative and transformative justice approaches teach us to do? In this conversation, when we're talking about violence and crime, I think it is important to note that many of the people who voted for Paul Vallas are the people who are not themselves impacted by the violence. As we began talking about policing and police investment during the election cycle, the diversion to crime became

a way to de-center those who have been most harmed by our public institutions, by our government and by the police department.

We need to center the families of victims of police violence, such as Rekia Boyd, Pierre Loury, Ronald "Ronnieman" Johnson, Laquan McDonald, Adam Toledo, Quintonio LeGrier and Bettie Jones, and so many more who we do not have the space to name.

We need to center the families of the survivors of torture, and we need to continue to re-platform the work of the Chicago Torture Justice Center and the Chicago Torture Justice Memorial, and how they are documenting and also working to heal from one of the worst institutionalized torture rings in America. We need to center the countless people who have been harassed, abused, hurt, harmed, mistreated and disrespected by the police.

We need to center the people who have been displaced: those students and teachers who had their schools closed. The people who had their public housing demolished. The people who were priced out of their homes and evicted. Those who were poisoned by harmful materials, whether it be from Chicago Housing Authority (CHA) or from other city institutions or from corporate institutions who profit from polluting the neighborhoods. Many people in Chicago have had their health diminished and their lives shortened, because the public responsibility was not taken to protect people from preventable harm.

Lastly, we need to center the communities that have been suffering from organized poverty and abandonment. Chicago has had some of the highest statistically documented, racially concentrated poverty in the country.

In Chicago, institutional harm has largely come out of CPD, CHA and CPS, and there have been people who have been organizing to address and acknowledge the harm.

There are also people in the Black political class who have aligned themselves with those who harm the Black community, and with the white supremacist base, in the name of capitalism, and self-interest. They endorsed Paul Vallas for mayor, and in doing so, aligned with white supremacist actors such as the Fraternal Order of Police (FOP) and billionaire Ken Griffin, who directly profits from the gun violence in Chicago while funding reactionary politicians. I want to name them. Bobby Rush, Jesse White, Roderick Sawyer, Sophia King, and Ja'Mal Green should no longer have viable careers in Black politics. Calling out their alignment as selling out the community should be part of the acknowledgement of harm, and part of the consequence of how we see them moving forward.

REVOLUTION IS NOT A SINGULAR EVENT...REVOLUTION IS A PROCESS.

As somebody who is committed to Black liberation on a multi-generational, lifetime basis, the Black Panthers in the Black radical tradition and liberation actually hold spiritual significance for me. Almost similar to how folks have saints or orishas, I have a spiritual connection to and reverence for them. So for Bobby Rush to betray that legacy and to collaborate with the folks who killed Fred Hampton, the folks who work to destroy that legacy and never want it to be taught in schools, I think that type of insincerity should make you no longer viable as a political figure in our community. And moving forward, as we see someone like Ja'Mal Green who is at a younger age working to come into prominence, we need to consider what our standards are and what we will allow.

Now, how do we hold the Johnson administration accountable? First, let's be clear: the election of Brandon Johnson is amazing and historically significant. But it is not a revolution. Revolution is not a singular event, a contest or a battle. Revolution is a process. Of course, the revolutionary process made this election possible. It is through the folks working for abolition and environmental justice and public education, who are actually trying to transform our society towards being healthy and meeting the needs of all life, that this moment was made possible.

On the campaign trail, Johnson made promises about police, policing and police investment that weren't aligned with an abolitionist framework. He walked back his previous statement on defunding the police being a political strategy, and said he wouldn't cut CPD's budget at all. I think, as strategic calculus, that made sense and can be understood. I actually don't know anybody who is demanding that he abolish the police department in his first term or his first 100 days. That is not the political reality we're at.

But the message that investment in policing is a path towards safety is just a false premise that actually supports our oppression. So even though it may have been needed strategically to defend against some political attacks, I think that messaging affirmed our opposition's values and principles.

Before the election, Brandon Johnson was not a well-known political figure. He did not take the traditional route of launching a campaign and then building a base; there was a base that had coalesced around a progressive political vision and was looking for someone to champion its platform. That base activated and made Brandon Johnson possible. So we have to continue to hold our expectations of ourselves to a higher level, and that includes holding Johnson to a higher standard as well.

How do we hold ourselves accountable and raise our expectations? We need higher expectations of ourselves, as people, as community members, as participants. We need higher expectations of our government and what it even means to govern, to provide resources, to even make laws. We need to have higher expectations of Brandon Johnson as an executive. We have selected him to be a representative leader with executive power over our collective resources. So within that, we have to be in the practice of what it means to hold a line to have a higher standard.

We also need to elevate our ideals. Dreaming of the impossible got us here. People thought it would not be possible in the electoral arena to talk about things like investing in non-police solutions to public safety, housing as a human right, education and mental health and wraparound services as things we could demand. But if it wasn't for the movement incubating those dreams and creating a compass and roadmap for achieving them, we actually wouldn't be able to have this conversation, and there would not be a Brandon Johnson administration about to take office.

Let us advocate for building a public infrastructure that centers the work that the community and movement modeled and seeded, such as practices of mutual aid, expanding access to free, healthy food, finding creative solutions to affordable public housing, reclaiming vacant land. Investments in collective wellness and protection, and the framing of proactive, restorative and transformative justice. What does it look like to publicly invest in community members checking on neighbors, or being trained in de-escalating conflict? How can we revive the spirit of Chicago's block club tradition? How can we bring the people to participate in creating the kind of public safety that played such an outsize role in the election?

Lastly, I want to emphasize that it wasn't just political strategy that built this community. It was really culture, creativity and humanity. So in terms of raising our standards, expectations and ideals, let's make more ambitious art. Let's make better art. We're not going to be able to address violence, poverty, bureaucracy or political corruption, if we are not nurturing our creative faculties. Art builds our humanity, and becoming more human builds our power. We have the opportunity to be more powerful.

In my first piece for *The TRiiBE* earlier this year, I asked you not to move in fear. I believe the counterbalance to that is to take the opportunity for bravery, and to be in the state of freedom-making. Freedom is a courageous act, and ours is a movement towards hope.

Photo by Darius
The

WE ARE THE FIRE

We are built from the ashes of the extinguished
From the blood of what couldn't be killed
A fire that will consume empires
Born as clenched fist
Survival made material
And our dreams will empty cages

by Kelly Hayes

ACKNOWLEDGMENTS

The *TRiiBE* is beyond grateful for our community of sponsors, readers, subscribers, mentors, contributors and supporters who breathe life into the work that we do. It is only through being in community with each and every one of you that we're able to uplift the stories and experiences of Black Chicagoans.

Thank you to **Haymarket Books** for seeing the importance of our 2021 Heritage Edition of the *TRiiBE Guide*, and partnering with us to distribute this 2023 reissue.

We'd also like to take a moment to give a special thanks to the following organizations and individuals who played a role in bringing our 2021 *TRiiBE Guide* to life.

2021 *TRiiBE GUIDE* SPONSOR

Chicago Beyond

ADDITIONAL SUPPORTERS

Business Leadership Council (BLC)
The Obsidian Collection
WROTE - A division of The Obsidian Collection Archives
Deeply Rooted Dance Theater
Goodman Theatre
Public Allies
Sisters in Cinema
Museum of Contemporary Art Chicago
Chicago Freedom School
OTV | Open Television
The Silver Room
Unapologetic Film
Resident Association of Greater Englewood (R.A.G.E.)

ADVISORY BOARD

Mr. Pemon Rami
Adam Morgan
Deborah Burns
Maya Rhodan
Dr. Elizabeth Todd-Breland
Jehoiada Zechariah Calvin
Marcia Walker-McWilliams
Kate Masur
Rosa Pineda

OUTREACH PARTNERS

Black Ensemble Theater
Kuumba Lynx
The Haitian American Museum of Chicago
The DuSable Black History Museum and Education Center
Workers Center for Racial Justice
South Side YMCA
Robust Coffee Lounge

Bessie Coleman Branch, Chicago Public Library
South Side Community Art Center
Teamwork Englewood
Build Bronzeville — The Bronzeville Incubator
Precious Blood Ministry of Reconciliation
Carter G. Woodson, Chicago Public Library
The #LetUsBreathe Collective

Principle Barbers
New Life Centers
BUILD, Inc.
Westside Justice Center
Austin Coming Together
Chicago Freedom School
Illinois Coalition for Higher Education in Prison - (Stateville Correctional Center and Cook County Department of Corrections)

Printed in the USA
CPSIA information can be obtained
at www.ICGtesting.com
JSHW072349021123
51171JS00001B/1